The Ulvila Murder:

The Truth Behind the Emergency Call

Niina Berg

THE ULVILA MURDER: THE TRUTH BEHIND THE EMERGENCY CALL

Translated by: August Translations

Cover by: Anna Elo

Published by: BoD · Books on Demand, Mannerheimintie 12 B, 00100
Helsinki, bod@bod.fi

Printed by: Libri Plureos GmbH, Friedensallee 273, 22763 Hamburg, Germany

ISBN: 978-952-80-6590-6

FOREWORD

Jukka Lahti was murdered at his home in the town of Ulvila in Finland on the night of 1 December 2006. Two years after the murder, the police had still not been able to determine who had murdered Lahti, and for this reason, the investigation returned to the beginning and to Lahti's wife, Anneli Auer, who was verifiably present at the time of the murder. The police had two distinct objectives in their investigation: to prove that only the members of the family were present at the time of the killing and to make Auer confess. That way Auer's guilt would be proven and no other evidence would be required against her. In reality, there was no other evidence.

The police built their investigation on the recording of the emergency call because by far its best characteristic was its ambiguity. As implied by the title, this book recounts the emergency call of the Ulvila murder and explains how and why it became the most important piece of evidence relating to it.

The book is based on the public material of the pre-trial investigation and of the trial itself, the courtroom recordings and the sentences passed in the case. I have also had the opportunity to familiarise myself with the classified material related to the case. The purpose of the book is to reflect on what is known about the Ulvila murder on the basis of the emergency call, on how the emergency call can be used to assist the criminal investigation and on what can be proven with it. I have studied expert statements issued about the emergency call and considered their trustworthiness and weight as evidence. I have sought to evaluate what can and cannot be reliably said of the case. The emergency call recording that is part of the trial material has been available on the internet for years for anyone to listen to, meaning that everyone has the opportunity to investigate the matter if they wish to do so.

The emergency call recording has been used as a piece of evidence to prove both the guilt and innocence of the mother who made the emergency call, but can it be used to reliably arrive at either conclusion? Is it possible to use the emergency call recording to prove that there were no outsiders present, or is the murderer's voice audible in the background? Can you trust the expert statements? Is the soundscape of the emergency call real or can you hear pre-recorded sounds in it? Is the emergency call recording identical to the original emergency call made to the emergency response centre?

What is the truth behind the Ulvila murder emergency call? All will be revealed on the pages of this book.

TRANSLATOR'S FOREWORD

The original Finnish transcriptions of the emergency call can be found in the appendices. Anything reproduced from the original transcriptions, including comments from the transcribers, has been kept in the format originally used as much as possible in order to preserve detail, resulting in some differences in portrayal in the book text. Any exceptions to this have been mentioned separately. In the body text, spoken lines quoted from the transcriptions are presented with the Finnish original first, followed by the English translation in brackets. For example: 'Mitä siellä nyt tapahtuu?' ('What is happening there now?'). In the lists highlighting certain parts of the transcriptions, the treatment of quoted spoken lines is explained separately. Comments of the transcribers are presented with the English translation only, unless there is a special need to include the Finnish original. Sound depictions are presented only in English in square brackets in a similar manner as they are presented in the original transcriptions. For example: [faint steps], [clatter]. Sounds, which depict screams, groaning and other kinds of non-verbal vocalisations, such as 'Auuu', 'Aii' and 'Öh', are presented in the translation as they are in the transcriptions.

1. THE ULVILA MURDER

An unusual homicide and its unusual investigation

Jukka Lahti was murdered at his home in the town of Ulvila in Finland during the night of 1 December 2006. He was accompanied by his wife and the four children of the family. The emergency response centre of the Satakunta region received an emergency call at 2.43 a.m. from Anneli Auer, wife of Jukka Lahti, who explained that an unidentified man had forced entry into their home and was attacking her husband with a knife. She had also been stabbed. The emergency call lasted four minutes and 20 seconds, during which time Lahti was killed. Auer left the phone at one point, and during this period the eldest child of the family, Amanda, then a 9-year-old girl, spoke to the emergency services. The police arrived at the scene approximately nine minutes after the beginning of the emergency call, but by then it was too late: Lahti was dead, and the perpetrator had managed to escape. The call was recorded on the system of the emergency response centre, and a copy of the emergency call recording was given to the police for the homicide investigation first thing in the morning.

According to Finland's national statistical institute Statistics Finland, the percentage of homicides solved in Finland is high every year, close to one hundred per cent, and only a very small number of homicides are left unsolved. In any other type of offence, the percentage solved is nowhere near the same level. This may create the impression that the police would be particularly skilled in solving homicides, but the truth is different – on average, a typical homicide in Finland is solved easily and quickly because the guilty party is often found at the crime scene, or can be named by other people who have been present, or the guilt is otherwise very evident in some other way. A quarter of the guilty turn themselves in to the police.

A typical homicide in Finland is a so-called manslaughter resulting from an argument under the influence, which means the homicide is heavily connected with the use of intoxicants. According to Statistics Finland and the Finnish Institute of Criminology and Legal Policy, in most cases, both parties are socially excluded, middle-aged substance-abusing men, and over 80 per cent of the killers and about 70 per cent of the victims are under the influence of alcohol or some other intoxicant at the time of the criminal act. Homicides are usually committed in private residences among familiar people drinking together using an edged weapon found in the household.

Even though the percentage of homicides solved is high and more effort is put into their investigation than into any other type of offence, a few homicides remain unsolved each year. The murder of Jukka Lahti was not a typical homicide because it was not preceded by the consumption of alcohol with the perpetrator. Instead, the perpetrator forced entry into the house at night with the intention of killing. Furthermore, the perpetrator was not identified and did not turn himself in. The murder of Jukka Lahti is one of over 200 homicides in Finland where the perpetrator remains unknown.

If the murder of Lahti was an unusual homicide, the pre-trial investigation was not quite standard either. To solve the crime, the police consulted a clairvoyant, used hypnosis and conducted a covert operation.

Next, I will recount in more detail a few more of the unusual things related to the pre-trial investigation.

Contamination. A bloody piece of firewood gathered from the murder site contained Lahti's DNA as well as DNA from the unidentified man, suspected to belong to the murderer. All those who were deemed suspects at the early stages of the investigation were tested, and most were eliminated from the investigation as soon as their DNA results arrived. This element of the investigation included a so-called mass testing of over 700 men, mainly people associated with Lahti's workplace – in his job, Lahti had participated in the redundancy process of hundreds of people, and initially the motive for the murder was thought to be personal revenge. The investigation soon discovered that Lahti had not been well-liked at his workplace. In addition, relatives told detectives that Lahti had received job-related threats.

When Anneli Auer was prosecuted for murder, another explanation had to be found for the above DNA results, and this is when it was suggested that the DNA could actually belong to anyone and originate from anywhere. According to the investigator in charge, Pauli Kuusiranta, the DNA could be from, for example, a mosquito: 'If a mosquito that has sucked itself full of blood is killed, it is likely that the place where it was killed will also contain DNA.'

It was not until seven years later that it was revealed that the DNA belonged to a forensic laboratory analyst at the National Bureau of Investigation (NBI, Finland). According to a new laboratory report, DNA contamination took place despite the fact that the analyst in question had not even worked in the laboratory areas where the piece of firewood had been kept and examined – the laboratory report presumed that the DNA had been transferred to the piece of firewood either via the air or the work equipment (e.g. a camera) used by staff collectively.

Humans have DNA in their blood, semen, skin cells, saliva, hair follicles, bones and teeth, as well as small amounts in their faeces and urine. None of these can transfer to another room by air. The piece of firewood examined was in the laboratory in December, which means the DNA could also not be from a mosquito. If the laboratory did indeed have a collectively-used camera, it would be possible that the analyst had sneezed near the camera or somehow accidentally got saliva on it, or that skin cells had been transferred onto it from their hands and remained there. The DNA would then have had to be transferred from the camera to the hands of another analyst who used the camera. Furthermore, this transfer process would then require that the second analyst must have touched the piece of firewood and transferred the DNA from their hands onto that. This sounds unbelievable, but it could also be true. It is possible that the murderer may have been disregarded in the investigation due to this mistake.

Calls to the City of Porvoo Police Station. One of the peculiarities in the case related to the 'Porvoo branch' of the investigation. During the murder investigation, it became clear that Lahti had made three phone calls to the extension number of the senior constable of the Porvoo Police Station in May 2006 (on 4, 8 and 10 May). This same number had called Lahti twice (on 19 June and 1 September). During the call Lahti made on 10 May, the username of an investigation secretary had logged into the police information system and conducted searches for information tagged with Lahti's name and personal identity code. The search terms included the dates 2006-04-29 and 2006-04-30 (in the format used by the police) as well as the codes P101 and 6590. Of these, 6590 is the Porvoo region code but there is no certainty what P101 is, it could even be a code relating to Lahti. On the basis of this, it can be deduced that the system was used for searching for information on a police matter in which Jukka Lahti would have been involved in one way or another which related to the Porvoo Police Station during the time period in question. I do not know the meaning of search code P101, and the police refused to tell it to me because according to them 'The information belongs to the emergency response centre's system and is part of the tactical and technical methods used by the police in the same manner as patrol identifiers and location data, which are classified information under section 24, subsection 1, paragraph 5 of the Act on the Openness of Government Activities'.

When asked about the matter (in 2008 and 2010), the senior constable expressed that he did not converse with Lahti or know him. If what he said was noted down correctly, this constable must have a remarkable memory for names – he remembers phone call conversations from years ago with people previously unfamiliar to him. The investigation secretary stated in her hearing (in 2012) that she did not know Lahti and did not remember answering Lahti's calls. According to the secretary, she had not answered the senior constable's phone, and she had also not called Lahti from the senior constable's phone because she had only ever used her own phone.

The police later informed the media that the senior constable whose extension number was called was off duty at the time when the phone calls were made. The question is: was this person actually on duty, nevertheless? The murder investigation material includes lists of police work shifts from the time period in question, and according to these, the senior constable was in fact working on both days when the phone in his personal use was used to call Lahti. A quick look at the work shift list makes it appear that the senior constable had been on leave on 10 May, which is precisely when searches were made into the police information system during Lahti's call. Upon closer examination of the work shift list, it can actually be seen that the time period marking at the top has been cut off, and that the list does not represent May 2006 but instead February–March 2009. This can be confirmed from the days and dates mentioned, as in 2009 the 28th day of the month is a Saturday and Sunday is the 1st of March. The work shift list had been received by fax from the investigation secretary of the Eastern Uusimaa Police Department on 27 February 2009 and its covering letter read only 'in reference to the phone conversation'. But what do the work shift lists of the Porvoo police from the year 2009 have to do with the Ulvila murder, a crime that took place over two years earlier?

The shift list for May 2006 would seem to be completely missing from the investigation material, even though, according to the covering letter, it has been delivered at the same time (in June 2008) with the June and September lists for 2006 which still remain present. At one point, I enquired after the whereabouts of this missing work shift list, and Detective Chief Inspector Erik Salonsaari reassured me that the police do also have the May 2006 work shift list, stored in a safe place.

A further investigation report dated 4 April 2011 reads as follows: 'The phone calls to the Porvoo Police Station and from there to Lahti's work cell phone have not been cleared up. However, nothing has emerged that would suggest these phone calls relate to the killing of Lahti.' The question is, how could anything have emerged when nothing was found out about the calls? According to their statement, the police do not know who answered Lahti's calls at the Porvoo Police Station and what Lahti wanted to discuss with the police, or who from the police called Lahti or what the reason was for those calls. None of Lahti's close relatives, friends or workmates were aware of any connections Lahti would have had in Porvoo itself or with the Porvoo police. This 'Porvoo branch' was left completely unresolved, but for some reason it was important for the police that it appeared that the senior constable in question had not been working during the most important phone call. Why was this so important? According to the senior constable, he knew nothing of the entire matter.

Secrecy. The material of the pre-trial investigation included almost none of the material gathered during the time of the first investigator in charge, Juha Joutsenlahti, and the existence of that material had been concealed. The concealed material included several documents that were important for solving the crime, such as details of the questioning of people associated with Lahti, and of people associated with Auer, expert statements, transcriptions made from the emergency call, police-made reconstructions and forensic investigations. No mention of the omitted material had been made in the pre-trial investigation report, and therefore the defence had no knowledge of their existence.

Oikeustoimittajat ry (the Finnish Association of Legal Journalists) later awarded the Sumuverho (or 'smoke screen') award to the Satakunta region police for this concealment of the majority of the pre-trial investigation material relating to the Ulvila murder. Their reasoning for the decision was that the police of Satakunta had withheld over 80 per cent of the pre-trial investigation reports and their attachments in a murder case that had received enormous attention. According to Oikeustoimittajat ry, this cover-up by the police seriously endangered both the legal safety of the accused and the right of the public to receive information. The cover-up was justified by the police as being to do with protection of privacy for all the parties concerned, but it still aroused a well-founded suspicion that the intention was also actually to cover mistakes and failures made by the police themselves.

This could be deduced, for example, from the fact that different versions had been made of the photograph appendix of the official pre-trial investigation report. The original version made by a technical investigator included a photograph that was important for the accused as it could be used to deduce that one of the police reconstructions had been made with incorrect measurements. However, someone had decided to keep this photograph secret and had replaced it with another unrelated one in the material received by the defence and the prosecution. The incorrectly-made reconstruction had been included in the pre-trial investigation report without any mention that the result did not correspond to reality.

It was pure chance that the replacement of this photograph was later revealed. If the police could modify the evidence to create untrue versions to suit their liking, what else could they do?

Endless investigation. The pre-trial investigation of the homicide ended a little after three years since the murder, on 13 January 2010. The case was transferred to the prosecutor who then brought murder charges against Auer. However, the criminal investigation by the police did not stop there – it continued throughout the entire legal proceedings, all the way to their conclusion. The prosecutor asked for further investigation 17 times, the last time as late as 2015.

The murder was argued in court for two full rounds of proceedings. The case was litigated twice in the Satakunta District Court, twice in the Vaasa Court of Appeal and then twice in the Supreme Court. In addition to the actual murder, the litigation also dealt with the handing over of the covert activity report to the defence, and this matter went all the way to the Supreme Court as well. The murder trials finally ended when the Supreme Court dismissed the application for leave to appeal by the prosecutors in 2015, and the acquittal of the Vaasa Court of Appeal remained legally binding.

2. USING AN EMERGENCY CALL AS A PIECE OF EVIDENCE IN A CRIMINAL CASE

What kind of proof is an emergency call?

The primary purpose of recording emergency calls is to record the conversation between the caller and the emergency response centre operator, but the recordings themselves can sometimes provide unique evidence of crimes. In the case of a homicide that takes place during a phone call to the emergency response centre, it is natural to utilise all the available information in the recording for the criminal investigation.

The Ulvila murder emergency call provided a lot of information. Among other things, the following was established: the time when the call was made, the duration of the call, the caller's immediate explanation of what had happened, the behaviour of the caller and how they had answered the operator's questions. The emergency call provided a basis for deducing different things, such as what happened in the house during the call, the time the victim was probably killed and how much time had elapsed between the start and end of the emergency call and the arrival of the police. The emergency call also made it possible to compare the crime scene and its traces with the caller's description of events and see if they corresponded.

Not all the sound information from the crime scene can be heard from the emergency call recording. It is naturally impossible to hear sounds on the recording that did not carry from the fireplace room of the house (a room commonly found in detached houses in Finland), which was also being used as the bedroom of the parents of the family, to the kitchen where the emergency call was made. The transmission of sound through the phone is influenced by the distance of the sound source from the phone receiver. The landline phone used to make the emergency call was located about 10–12 metres from the actual crime scene, which was the fireplace room. Then, of the sounds that reached the phone only a proportion were transmitted forward through the phone call.

In the normal operation of a telephone, the microphone is optimised to best transmit sounds that are coming from nearby – in other words speech directed to the phone – and correspondingly to fade out other sounds. For this reason, very faint sounds or sounds coming from a further distance do not necessarily transmit through the phone at all. Loud background sounds may still be transmitted but could be much fainter than the original sound in the resulting recording.

Simultaneous sounds may also cover each other in a manner leading to some sounds not being audible at all or only being partially heard. The voice spoken into the microphone can cover up sounds from the background quite efficiently. The direction of the phone's receiver also affects the sound being recorded – when the receiver is pointed in the direction of the source of the sounds, they are heard more clearly compared to when the receiver is pointed away.

The frequency band of a telephone line is limited with filters to about 300–3,500 hertz. Within this range are the frequencies important for understanding speech, that is 500–2,500 hertz. Frequencies that are lower and higher than standard phone filtering are filtered out, and the frequency band of a telephone will start to muffle sounds below 300 hertz and above 2,500 hertz. Because of this filtering some of the sound information is left outside of this range. Very low thump sounds and correspondingly very high glass clinking and chinking sounds, for example, are not transmitted to the other end in a phone call because of the filtering and so they may be neither audible nor recorded. Filtering may also remove a part of the characteristics of a sound. When, for example, high tones are not recorded within the high-pitched clink of glass, the sound resulting may be heard completely different in a recording and, for instance, it may end up sounding like a clicking sound.

The phone calls made to the emergency response centre during the murder were recorded into the NiceLog system. This system recorded the sound in a compressed file format and the compression process itself also lost part of the audio signal. Parts of the call that have no significance for auditory perception can be left out of the recording of the signal during this process. In addition, at the time, sound was still being recorded into monophonic recording format, which meant that simultaneous sounds got mixed with each other.

Humans are capable of detecting distances from and directions of different sounds from their environment rather well. To some extent, it is possible to perceive how far away the sounds heard in the recording are in relation to the phone. However, it is not possible to determine any accurate distances on the basis of the recording; nor is it possible to determine the directions that the recorded sounds are coming from using the monophonic recording.

Because of the location of the phone, its microphone, the position of the phone's receiver and the filtering of the telephone line as well as because of the recording system, it was part of the character of the resulting emergency call recording that some of the sounds heard in the background of the phone call in the actual situation were not recorded on the final recording and cannot be heard. For example, at 3:11 minutes into the emergency call, Auer says 'nyt hiljeni' ('now it's silent') – heard by myself and also transcribed by Niemi and Sihvonen – which means she cannot hear her husband's voice anymore. She either becomes aware at that moment that Lahti's voice cannot be heard anymore, or Lahti actually becomes silent only at that moment. After 2:28 minutes into the recording, you cannot hear the voice or any sounds that would clearly be made by Lahti. However, several clunks can be still heard after this instant of time. Lahti's groaning sounds could have been so faint that they were not transmitted by the phone's microphone, even if they might have been audible to a human ear in the actual house. The sounds of the victim may otherwise have been obscured by the speech of the caller and the emergency response centre operator. It is possible that Auer had heard her husband groaning for a longer time than what can be heard in the emergency call recording, or perhaps she had another reason to say what she said.

Auer described that there was loud noise, caused by the sounds of fighting and the victim's groans, coming from the fireplace room. As it stands, this loud noise is not conveyed fully in the emergency call recording. In addition to the groaning of the victim, a lot of other sounds can be heard in the background; however, these background sounds are not audible as loud noise in the recording. It should be remembered nevertheless that because of the distance of the phone from the fireplace room, all the sounds that have been recorded from there must have been quite loud, otherwise they would not have been recorded at all. In the actual house, people would have been surrounded by a different soundscape than the one transmitted through the phone call and then to the recording. The fact that some sounds cannot be heard in the emergency call recording cannot be used to reliably conclude that such sounds were not heard in the actual situation. To summarise, the people who were present at the time of the incident would have heard a different, more diverse and louder soundscape than those who listen to the events from the recording.

Subjectivity of auditory perceptions

Sounds can naturally be examined best by listening to them. At the time of the incident, emergency call recordings were generally rather poor in quality, and that is true of this case as well. The most reliable perceptions can be made if a recording is listened to with headphones in peace in an undisturbed and quiet space. Different audio processing software can also be used to improve sound quality when examining sounds. The software can be used, for example, to remove unnecessary and distracting noise and crackles, to amplify weaker and more silent sounds into more audible ones, to muffle loud noises, to slow down the sound velocity, etc. When drawing conclusions, it must be taken into consideration that modification and improvement of sound quality can considerably change the sound and the tone quality from what they were originally. With the help of audio processing software, it is also possible to make the audio visible and examine the sound waves as images.

All studies based on human senses are always subjective, and this includes audio research as well. Auditory perceptions are always individual firstly because of the level of accuracy of one's sense of hearing and secondly because the hearing experience depends on the listener's personal interpretation. This interpretation can be affected, sometimes strongly, by the listener's background information on the matter as well as their own previous experiences, presumptions and ability to comprehend. Therefore, when a piece of evidence related to a murder investigation is in question in particular, the matter should be examined as neutrally as possible to determine objective truth, independent of any personal views and intentions brought by the listener.

When striving for neutrality, it is of primary importance to recognise and be aware of one's own presumptions regarding the matter at hand. This helps ensure that personal views do not direct the interpretation of the recorded sounds towards one's own assumptions or make the interpretation of the sounds fit these assumptions better. Because audio research is based mainly on subjective observation and interpretation of what is heard, the significance of the reasoning around this interpretation is emphasised – in other words, on what grounds a certain sound is interpreted to have been produced by a certain person, or on what grounds a certain sound is interpreted to have been created by a certain thing or event.

The transcriptions made from the emergency call recording in the Ulvila case should therefore be approached with critical consideration because auditory experiences are always primarily every individual's personal experiences. If a transcription accompanying the call is made by someone else, then this may also affect one's own auditory experience, especially regarding unclear sounds – if a sound you are listening to is unclear, but the transcription you are reading of it at the same time is clear, you may start to 'hear what you read' instead of what you would have heard without the transcription. Sounds may be written in the transcription correctly and the hearing experience may therefore be similar for different people, but this is not always the case – sometimes it may lead to the so-called McGurk effect, that is, an illusion based on an interaction between hearing and vision in speech perception. This illusion is experienced when visual and auditory information is processed in the brain simultaneously and interpreted incorrectly. It is most likely to be experienced when a person is receiving poor-quality auditory information and good-quality visual information at the same time. Many people have surely come across tests based on this phenomenon on the internet, such as the 'green needle / brainstorm' test (taken from a recorded toy review which explores very similar sounding words). In this test, the word spoken sounds very close to a different word, and it often happens that you hear the voice clearly say the word you are already looking at or thinking of – therefore, if you have the word 'green needle' in mind, you will hear that, but if you are thinking of the word 'brainstorm', the acoustic cues that fit it are stronger and you will hear that instead even if the recorded voice is exactly the same in both cases.

Prior information on the matter may therefore affect the perception of a sound, especially when a person believes the information is coming from a reliable source or does not question the provided information for one reason or another. Sensory perceptions may also be distorted in cases that arouse powerful emotions (fear, disgust, hatred). Powerful emotions can in addition affect the brain's function and, for example, when in a state of fear, people's perceptions can be very different from those occurring in a state of calm.

I have personal experience of how prior information of a matter may affect perception, even if the information is incorrect and contradicts presented information. At the time of the August 2017 terrorist attack in Turku, Finland, I received a link to a video from an acquaintance of mine with an accompanying note that said the video was about terrorists running down the street shouting 'Allahu akbar'. This aroused strong emotions in me, and I was not in a state of mind to question the information that I had been provided in the video's content. In the video, I saw men of foreign origin running down a street; I assumed they were the said terrorists and heard them shouting 'Allahu akbar'. I found out later that the men in the video were not terrorists, but instead they were trying to catch the terrorist and warned people of a man with a knife by shouting 'Varo varokaa' ('Look out, be careful'). When I watched the video again, I could clearly hear the warning shouts and was not able to hear the religious shout any more in any way. My auditory perception was also surely partly altered by the way the video image seemed to fit the prior information received, making it easier for my auditory perception to adjust to this provided information.

Prior information and emotions may also have affected perceptions in the statements regarding the Ulvila murder emergency call. Those who issued the statements would surely have trusted the information provided by the police, and in addition a brutal homicide taking place in the home of a family with children is enough to arouse strong emotions in anyone.

From the beginning, a reasonably widespread agreement has prevailed regarding the words spoken on the phone between the emergency response centre operator, the caller and the child present in the house who also spoke on the phone. This is most likely because their speech was recorded sufficiently clearly to be heard properly, leaving less room for ambiguity. The dialogue on the phone is also mostly a logical conversation that includes elements familiar to everyone, making it easier to understand the speech. However, the sounds heard in the background of the call have caused significant differences in opinion. These background sounds are fainter and less clear and, because of this, already fundamentally more difficult to hear. Many of the background sounds heard in the recording are broken up because they are partly covered by the words spoken directly into the receiver by whoever is on the phone. This makes it more difficult to perceive the whole of the soundscape. The background sounds are also more difficult to understand and more unfamiliar as sounds. For anyone, recognising personally unfamiliar sounds is naturally always more difficult than recognising sounds which are more familiar and everyday.

Various sounds can be heard in the background of the emergency call, and it is impossible to say with certainty what or who has created them, so they leave a lot of room for speculation, assumption and interpretation. Therefore, it is difficult if not impossible to identify the background sounds reliably. Conclusions based on sounds can only be made reliably for those sounds that are clearly audible and recognisable. Speculations made on the basis of speech that is unclear or has been only partially recorded, or other sounds that are unclear or hard to recognise, cannot be considered as having the same significance when they regard matters as serious as murder investigations.

Presentation of evidence by experts

Presentation of evidence is a central part of a criminal trial and used by both parties to prove their version of the progress of events is correct. In the judicial system in Finland, evidence is assessed on the basis of free evaluation of evidence, which means the court has the right to free discretion of the probative force of the presented evidence. The court must make an overall assessment of the evidence but also justify its ruling by giving reasons separately for the reliability of each piece of evidence supporting the judgement. The statement of reasons by the court permits the subsequent evaluation of a ruling that has been made on free discretion. The obligation to provide a statement of reasons applies to all evidence evaluation, including determining the probative value of an expert statement, and it is emphasised especially in situations where parties involved in the trial have referred to contradicting expert statements.

Court judges have usually gained the general education of a lawyer and therefore vast knowledge of other special fields cannot be expected from them. The presentation of evidence by experts often has an important role to play in a criminal trial in cases where general knowledge and life experience are not sufficient for the basis of a ruling. In principle, expert statements are considered to have a high probative value when they are given by a person with knowledge and experience in the special field in question. In an ideal situation such a statement would be a great help for the court in solving the case as truthfully as possible. Because the presentation of evidence by experts can have an essential impact on the court decision, its reliability plays an important role. The possibility available for a court to verify the truthfulness of a statement is usually limited, which means that utilising expert knowledge in a criminal trial is not without problems. The situation can be jeopardising for the legal protection of the accused in particular if the evidence presented by the experts during a criminal trial has no scientific basis, or has non-existent probative value in other ways.

The emergency call recording in this case has been used as evidence to prove both the guilt and the innocence of Anneli Auer, the person who made the emergency call. However, whether it can be used to arrive reliably at either conclusion is questionable. Several dozen expert statements have been provided to accompany the emergency call by the police, the prosecution and the defence. The statements have in many areas been contradictory or have invalidated each other. The recording has also been studied twice by the Federal Bureau of Investigation (FBI) in the United States. The Finnish police posed the same questions regarding the examination of the recording to both the FBI and the forensic laboratory of the National Bureau of Investigation (NBI) of Finland, but nevertheless many of the examination results have been polar opposites. One expert finds that it is impossible to state anything reliable of a given issue, whereas another expert presents absolutely certain conclusions from the same material. How trustworthy can we consider these kinds of expert statements to be?

The starting point in evaluating the trustworthiness of an expert statement is to examine the competence of the expert. An expert differs from a layman by having special knowledge of a certain field through education and experience and will also know how to apply this information when making deductions. An expert will also know how to evaluate the investigated subject critically and know how to give reasons for their competence and conclusions to outsiders in an understandable manner. In addition to their specialist know-how, honesty and neutrality must be demanded of an expert witness and the examination they provide, along with consideration of alternative perspectives and a professionally reflective attitude towards their own methods and motives.

The Forensic Laboratory of the NBI is part of the police, and its services are not available to a person suspected or accused of a crime. This can be a problem in regard to the neutrality of the expert statements it produces. When an expert receives their assignment already during the pre-trial investigation, they will unavoidably approach the case from the police's viewpoint. It is not easy to consider this kind of expert independent and neutral, at least from the standpoint of the defence.

Experts used by the police should always present their deductions as probabilities instead of absolute truths. The presentation of evidence by an expert appointed by the defence or the prosecution carries an increased risk that the expert chooses the side of the party that has appointed them, which in turn would affect what they emphasise within their statement. The expert may develop, perhaps unconsciously, a need to please the person who has requested the statement. This may then manifest itself, for instance, in their giving a statement on a matter where in reality it is impossible to provide any reliable assessment. It may also, for example, lead to the presentation of deductions as certain and as the only options, even if they were not. Experts in this situation must be aware of the limitations and margins of error of the information they present and be able to evaluate whether the information can be applied to the situation in question. A good expert takes into account all possible realistic alternatives in their evaluation and does not have only one option they aim to ascertain. Experts must not speculate or make strong statements merely on the basis of impressions they have arising from a subject.

Knowledge based on empirical expertise differs from scientific knowledge, and its reliability is even harder to evaluate. Empirical knowledge can also be based on erroneous deduction. Often the phenomena that people have dealings with more frequently feel more common to them, even if this is not necessarily true in reality. When these personal experiences are used to make overgeneralised conclusions, a fallacy is created. Fallacies may also be created if one seeks confirmation for one's own beliefs from the subject that is being observed. In this case, the observer reinforces their own impression, which may have been originally false, with their own action. One of the problems of empirical knowledge is that special and unusual events stick in people's minds the best, which means that an unusual phenomenon may be perceived as normal and cause-effect factors are connected incorrectly.

Even if an auditory perception intrinsically relates to a person's subjective observation, the deductions of an expert conducting sound examination must nevertheless not be based on intuition, guesswork or personal opinions. Professional authority must never be used to present opinions that rest on the expert's feelings or impressions, and the presentation of evidence by experts which does not fulfil qualitative criteria has little probative value. Personal opinions provided by an expert cannot be considered to have any more value than opinions from a layman, and a feeling that a person gets from a certain matter is completely unnecessary information whether the person is an expert or not. Such an opinion cannot help a court of law. Information given in the role of an expert can have a significant effect on the outcome of the judgment, and therefore personal opinions and speculations presented as expert statements may, in the worst-case scenario, mislead the court in the evaluation of the evidence.

Listed below are the experts and expert authorities which have examined the Ulvila murder emergency call recording and given statements on the matter, either in the pre-trial investigation or in the trials.

Experts and expert authorities used by the police/prosecution:

- Tuija Niemi, Licentiate in Philosophy, sound analyst with the National Bureau of Investigation (NBI) Forensic Laboratory (I'm referring to her with the name Niemi, even though her surname in the early years of the case was Niemi-Laitinen)
  Niemi made two transcriptions (in 2006 and 2009) and different filtered versions of the emergency call recording. She has also given dozens of statements relating to the emergency call, been involved in making sound reconstructions of it and been heard as an expert witness in court.
- Pirkko Lahti, Licentiate in Philosophy, psychologist, psychotherapist
  Lahti gave a statement during the pre-trial investigation about Auer's behaviour during the emergency call and was heard as an expert witness about the same subject in court.
- Lasse Nurmi, Master of Social Sciences, psychologist, specialist of behavioural science with the NBI, Finland
  Nurmi gave a statement about Auer's behaviour during the emergency call during the pre-trial investigation.

- Mika Sihvonen, Licentiate in Philosophy, senior assistant in the Hypermedia Laboratory, University of Tampere
  During the pre-trial investigation, Sihvonen wrote a transcription (2008) of the emergency call and separated possible sounds from it made by the perpetrator.
- Federal Bureau of Investigation
  The FBI made a filtered version of the emergency call in 2009 and answered specific questions asked by the Finnish police regarding the emergency call recording in 2012.
- A team assembled by the prosecutor in 2015 included, in addition to Tuija Niemi, the following people:
  - Raine Ampuja, conductor, composer
  - Tapio Lokki, Professor of the Department of Media Technology, Aalto University
  - Otto Romanowski, composer, senior lecturer in the Department of Music and Technology, Sibelius Academy
  - Mikko Raita, music producer

  This team mainly examined the emergency call recording at 1:57–2:11 minutes but answered questions from the police about other aspects of the call as well.

Experts used by the defence
- Risto Hemmi, Master of Science (Technology), Chief Executive Officer of Finnvox Studios
  Hemmi made his own filtered version of the emergency call recording and gave his opinion on, among other things, the question regarding the premade recording and the specific sounds heard on the actual recording. He was also heard as an expert witness in court.

- Micke Nyström, sound designer, sound specialist, Chief Executive Officer of Boomout Oy

  Nyström gave his opinion on the examination methods used by Ampuja's team and the conclusions the team made. Nyström also analysed a few of the sounds in the background and a few of the sounds made by the alleged outside perpetrator in the recording.
- Pekka Santtila, Doctor of Psychology, Professor of the Department of Applied Psychology, Åbo Akademi University

  Santtila examined, among other things, the behaviour of Auer and of the child present during the emergency call in accordance with a model developed in the United States. He was heard as an expert witness in court.
- Jukka Alihanka, Doctor of Medicine and Surgery, adjunct professor, composer/lyricist

  Alihanka made a statement on Auer's respiratory rate during the emergency call, among other aspects of it, and was also heard in court.

I describe these experts and expert authorities and their statements further later in this book according to their role in establishing details of the case.

3. SCENE OF THE EVENT AND DESCRIPTIONS OF THE EVENT

Scene of the event

The murder took place in an area of detached houses on Tähtisentie, a street in the town of Ulvila, in the Satakunta region, Finland. Whoever the murderer is, they broke the window glass in the door leading from the backyard decking into the fireplace room of the house and entered through the opening. The struggle between the murderer and Jukka Lahti occurred in the fireplace room. The murderer did not move elsewhere in the house and left through the same broken window in the back door that they had used to enter. This means the actual crime scene of the murder was the fireplace room of the house, which was also being used as the bedroom by the parents of the family.

Auer called the emergency number from a landline phone, next to a big pile of various papers located on the kitchen worktop. The distance from the phone to the location of the homicide scene in the fireplace room was about 12 metres. Auer related that during the emergency call, she went to peek into the fireplace room twice from the boundary between the living room and the fireplace room, roughly ten metres from the phone. Auer further related that she escaped the killer by going across the living room into the draught lobby and out of the front door.

The most important locations regarding the emergency call have been marked on the floor plan of the house below. These include the crime scene (i.e. the fireplace room), the location of the phone in the kitchen, the draught lobby and the front door. The appendices at the end of the book contain a more detailed floor plan made by Technical Investigator Matti Mäkinen; this plan shows the location of furniture, places where the bloody pieces of firewood and the knife used as the instrument of the crime were found, and also the location of the victim.

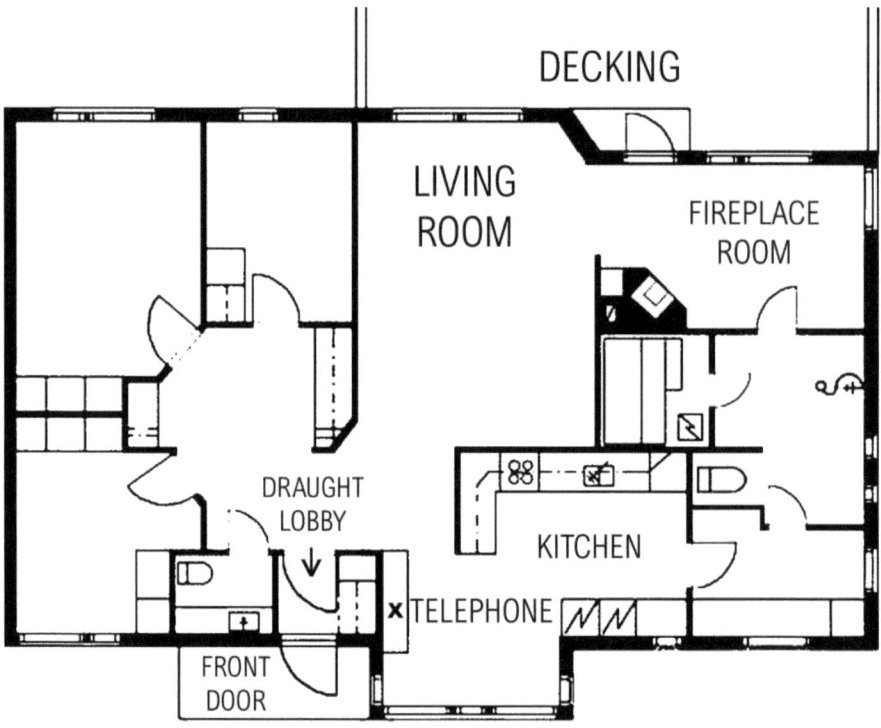

Floor plan of the house, with the location of the landline phone.

(Translator's note: a *draught lobby* is a small room built after the front door to reduce draught in houses in the Nordic countries. The Finnish word for this room, 'tuulikaappi', literally means 'wind cabinet'. Nowadays, front doors are tighter and they have better seals so draught lobbies are not built as often anymore.)

Anneli Auer's personal account

This book is concerned mainly with the emergency call — the most important piece of evidence for the prosecution — and does not go through other evidence in detail. However, in order to understand the whole, we must examine the descriptions of the offence that Auer was charged with and the role of the emergency call in relation to other presentations of evidence in broad outline and at different stages of the court proceedings. The text is based on Auer's account in the interviews and trials.

According to Auer's account, Lahti was murdered by a man from outside the family who was dressed in dark clothes and unfamiliar to her. This man forced entry into the house by breaking the window glass of the back door. Auer has related that the events on the night of the murder proceeded as follows: the couple woke up due to hearing noise at night as someone was breaking the window in the back door. Pieces of glass flew in from the window. Auer stayed in bed, but Lahti stood up and moved closer to the back door, which led to the decking. After a moment, someone entered through the broken window and attacked Lahti. Auer tried to intervene but was stabbed in the chest with a knife and fled from the fireplace room.

Auer saw her eldest child, her daughter Amanda, in the hall and told her there was a killer in the house, ordering the children to run outside and opening the front door of the house. After this she went into the kitchen to call the emergency services. It can be heard in the emergency call recording that Auer starts the call by saying 'Tääl on joku tappaja, tulkaa nopeesti!' ('There's a killer here, come quickly!') and then continues with 'Joku tuli ikkunast sisään' ('Someone came in through the window'). The emergency response centre operator calms the caller down, asks for the address and then asks 'Mitä siellä nyt tapahtuu?' ('What is happening there now?'). Auer responds, 'Joku tuli ikkunast sisää ja hakkaa puukol mun miestäni, muaki on hakattu' ('Someone came in through the window and is stabbing my husband with a knife, I've been stabbed too').

After this, the emergency response centre operator was temporarily off the phone line and nothing was heard from the emergency response centre for a while. At the same time, sounds of fighting and Lahti's cries of agony were coming from the fireplace room. Auer decided to go and see what was going on in the fireplace room but then remembered that the operator had asked her to stay on the phone. You can hear in the recording that Auer then asks her daughter to come to the phone and says '...Mä meen kattoo tonne' ('...I'm gonna go look there'), adding that she has called the police, and they have asked her to stay on the line. Auer related that she then went to have a look in the fireplace room where she saw the killer assaulting her husband. Then the killer went to attack Auer and she ran away across the living room, going into the draught lobby and all the way outside through the front door of the house to the porch. When she found that the killer had not followed her, she returned back inside again.

After a moment, Auer went to look into the fireplace room for a second time, but the killer turned towards her once more and Auer again ran away. The killer did not follow Auer more than a few steps this time either before going back to continue the attack on Lahti. After this, Auer returned to the phone. In the recording, Auer can be heard explaining:

'Mä juoksin äske ulos, jos mä meen sinne, se lähtee juoksee mun perää, se meni takas ja se aikoo tappaa mun mieheni, se oli äske viel hengis' ('I ran outside a moment ago, if I go there, he's gonna start running after me, he went back and he's gonna kill my husband, he was still alive a moment ago').

After the emergency call had ended, a police patrol then phoned Auer. Auer tried to move through the living room to go and see her husband, but there was a lot of broken glass around the doorway to the fireplace room, so she instead went around to look in through the shower room door. Auer attempted to feel her husband's pulse through the crack in the door but could only reach his shoulder. At this point Lahti was lying on the floor and looked lifeless. Auer then went outside to wait for the ambulance and police patrol.

On the basis of traces found at the crime scene, the police were able to quickly deduce that the perpetrator, whoever it was, had to be covered in a great deal of blood after the killing. This is a matter in which all have reached the same conclusion later in the investigation as well. The only prints with blood leading from the victim passed through the broken window and out onto the decking. In the living room, only one bloody mark made by the edge of the sole of a shoe was found. This was considered as a print made by the perpetrator possibly turning at the point when they had followed Auer for a few steps and then turned back to the victim. There was a muddy shoe print on the plastic chair lifted in front of the broken window outside, with a tread pattern that was identical to the bloody shoe prints. This was considered a possible print made by the perpetrator during their entry.

It was obvious that a person covered in a lot of blood had exited through the broken window. A partial bloody shoe print had been left on a pair of trousers draped over a chest next to the back door inside the house. There was also a wipe mark from a bloody sleeve on the wall above the chest. Drops of blood had flown onto the outer walls of the house and fallen onto the decking. There were also marks from a bloody dotted glove on the outside doorpost and the decking had bloody shoe prints. Judging from these traces, the window glass had been broken from the outside. The curtain had marks on the side that had been against the glass, i.e. pointing outward. The triple-paned window had broken from the left upper corner from the outside in such a way that the outer pane had broken the most, the middle pane a little less and the inner pane the least.

Auer herself was not bloody, apart from the blood stain which resulted from her own injury (the knife stab wound to the chest). The shower room of the house was dry and unused, meaning no one had washed there recently. Auer did not have any other injuries or bruises in addition to the stab wound and a few wounds from the pieces of glass on the ground to the soles of her feet. The investigations found no signs that Auer would have been the perpetrator. Auer's DNA was not found in samples taken from under Lahti's nails or from his clothes, nor from the pieces of firewood or the knife retrieved from the scene of the event. A lot of mottled brown synthetic fibres were found from the crime scene but their origin could not be solved. They were found on the victim, from the fireplace room and the window edges as well as from the decking. These fibres were not found on the red t-shirt worn by Auer.

Auer talked about an outside killer in the emergency call and related the same to the police. The eldest child of the family also reported that she had seen this person from behind as they left the house through the broken window. None of the facts in the forensic investigation contradicted the stories given by Auer and her daughter. The house search did not find anything else relating to the murder, such as bloody clothes or gloves, shoes matching with the shoe prints, the source of the mottled brown fibres or another instrument of the crime. At first, the police considered it likely that the murderer was a male from outside the family who had forced entry into the house by breaking the window of the back door. Three years later, the police were convinced that the murderer was Auer and that she had disguised the murder to make it appear to have been carried out by an outsider.

Descriptions of the murder in court

The prosecution demanded that Auer should be convicted of murder and presented the following description of the criminal act charged to the court (the translation has kept the tense used in the original description):

2010–2011. *After a mutual argument, Anneli Auer has killed her spouse Jukka Lahti in the manner detailed below.*

After Lahti returned from a business trip at around 11 p.m., an argument came about between the spouses, originating already from previous disagreements. This also led to a physical altercation by both sides. Worsening of the argument has led to the use of pieces of firewood and a kitchen knife as weapons used to strike each other. The latter weapon has been used by Jukka Lahti to jab Auer once in the chest, causing her a bleeding wound.

After Auer has at some stage gained control of the knife she has stabbed Lahti twice in his side, in addition to wounding Lahti's arms and hands, and stabbed him once in the armpit area in a manner causing the blade of the knife to reach a depth of 11–20 cm in the body with every strike.

The stabs to the side and the armpit area have caused Jukka Lahti several bleeding wounds and the loss of his ability to function. He has also most likely lost consciousness, at which point Auer has believed she has killed her spouse.

After this, by breaking the window and by making bloody shoe prints also outside of the decking area door, Auer has disguised the situation to make it appear that an outsider had forced entry into the house through the window and carried out the above criminal act on Jukka Lahti.

Lahti had, however, not died from Auer's previous stabbing but regained consciousness at some stage and started to groan heavily. To prevent her child, who was out of bed, from seeing the completion of the criminal act, Auer has called the emergency response centre and ordered her child to remain on the phone while she herself has gone into the bedroom, where she has hit Jukka Lahti, who was lying on the floor, twice on the face and head with a heavy object, causing his immediate death as a result of a blow that had crushed his skull. After this, Auer returned to the phone.

Because Auer has first caused multiple severe and painful injuries to Lahti with the knife and, without seeking help, allowed him to suffer for a long period of time before completing the criminal act, and because Lahti has been in a defenceless state, the criminal act has been committed in a particularly brutal and cruel manner. In addition, taking into consideration that the couple's mutual children have been awake at the time of the event, hearing as well as partially seeing their father's death struggle, the criminal act must be considered a murder when evaluating the wider picture.

In the first full round of the legal proceedings (2010–2011), the prosecution presented a description of the crime (as above) that suggested Auer had killed her spouse after the couple had had an argument and then disguised the surroundings to make them suggest an outside perpetrator. According to the charge, the homicide had been committed in two parts. Before making the emergency call, the prosecution claimed Auer had injured Lahti with the knife and then set up traces pointing to an outside perpetrator, for example by breaking the window and making bloody shoe prints both inside the house and outside on the decking. During the emergency call, they suggested she had gone on to kill her husband by hitting him on the head with a heavy object.

The prosecution used the emergency call recording as evidence to prove that Auer was guilty of murder. According to them, the emergency call recording excluded any possibility of an outside perpetrator. No sounds referring to an outsider could be heard on the recording, and this proved there was no outside perpetrator in the house. The prosecution proposed that there was a sound in the recording proving that the homicide had been made during the emergency call. Furthermore, the prosecution claimed that it could be heard on the recording that Auer had said a phrase referring to killing, and that Auer had been away from the phone at the moment when Lahti had received the fatal blows. It was also suggested by the prosecution that the recording indicated that Auer had been wearing shoes, and that this proved she had been out of bed for a long time.

The Satakunta District Court ruled that Anneli Auer was guilty of murder. The judgment found that evidence with the highest probative value was that of the testimony from witness and sound analyst Tuija Niemi and the emergency call recording itself, as well as the conclusion drawn from them that there was no outsider in the house during the call.

The Vaasa Court of Appeal, however, evaluated the evidence differently and dismissed the charge. Their judgement found that the only facts that supported the charge were that no speech from an outside perpetrator could be heard in the recording, that there were no clear sounds of fighting, walking on glass or of someone leaving, and, in particular, the fact that the fatal blow had been given during the call at a stage when the accused was not on the phone. According to the Court of Appeal, the absence of these sounds did not exclude the possibility of an outside perpetrator because the killing had still taken place during the emergency call and walking on glass should have created sounds no matter who the perpetrator was. The Court of Appeal concluded that the absence of sounds in the recording probably occurred because the sounds had not actually been recorded. The account of Risto Hemmi, CEO of Finnvox Studios and with a long experience of working in the sound industry, showed that sounds could still be heard in the background of the call after the accused had returned to the phone, and this indicated that an outside perpetrator could have been in the house.

2011–2012. The prosecution applied for leave to appeal the ruling from the Supreme Court and proposed that the case had new evidence that could not have been referred to previously. The prosecution's new evidence was based on the fact that nearly five years after the murder Auer's son, who was seven years old at the time of the crime, had begun to relate the events of the night differently compared to his previous account.

The child had now related that he had woken up on the night of his father's murder to the sound of a bang and had listened from behind the door of his room to what was happening in the other parts of the house. He had heard that his mother and eldest sister were awake and that they were whispering to each other and moving around the house, and that he heard them opening and closing doors during this. According to the child's impression, his mother had gone out of the front door. After this, the child thought he had heard breaking and rattling sounds of plates from the direction of the living room and fireplace room, which he had later associated with the breaking of the window in the door leading to the decking. He had then heard the sounds of a door opening and later closing, as well as several sounds he believed came from blows, followed by cries and groans from his father that were growing constantly stronger. After these sounds had stopped, the child had heard clicks and rewinding sounds which he believed to have come from the family's cassette player. After this, the sounds from his father had begun again, but seemed to sound identical to the way he had heard them previously, as if he was hearing them right from the beginning again. Then, the child had heard his mother making a phone call. Right after the call had ended, he had heard his mother's steps and a click from the cassette player. Soon after this, paramedics and the police had arrived at the house. Auer's son said he had not heard any sounds pointing to a person outside the family during this entire time.

In addition, the child stated that his mother and elder sister had spoken to each other and planned the killing of his father before it had taken place. The mother and elder sister had used boards to make frames, to which they had fixed brown towels that they had had for a long time and, according to the account of the child, these constructions had been used as protective shields during his father's murder. The child also recounted that about two weeks earlier, and again about two days before his father's murder, his mother had told him that he did not need to worry if he heard some nasty or strange sounds at night. He also said that his elder sister had been drawing pictures of the killing of their father before the murder occurred.

The prosecution proposed that this new presentation of evidence showed that sounds caused by the killing of the victim had been pre-recorded and played from a tape recorder during the emergency call, and that the brown towels from the household had been used as protection during the homicide, explaining the origin of the earlier unidentified brown fibres found at the crime scene. According to this new presentation of evidence, the accused had been planning the killing of her husband in the course of the year 2006. In addition to the child's account, the prosecution had a new statement from the Forensic Laboratory of the National Bureau of Investigation, and this also stated that part of the sounds heard in the emergency call recording could have possibly come from a recording that had been made earlier and then played during the call.

At this point, claims were even made that the murder was about satanism. The prosecution alleged that there had been inverted crosses made by stab wounds on Jukka Lahti's shoulders and that his ashes and blood had been used in rituals.

In its decision, the Supreme Court considered that the new evidence referred to a possible course of events that had not been used in evaluating the case previously and that it deviated significantly from the starting point which had been the basis for the judgments passed by the lower courts. For this reason, the Supreme Court reversed the previous judgments and ordered the case to be retried in the Satakunta District Court.

2013–2015. The prosecution's primary description of the criminal act charged remained the same during the second full round of the legal proceedings, even if the new round was argued to the Supreme Court specifically because of the new presentation of evidence. This suggested the murder had been planned in advance and the victim's groaning in the background of the emergency call originated from a recording that had been made earlier. However, it almost seemed that the prosecution was also not personally convinced by the new presentation of evidence and did not dare to trust that it would succeed, as they preferred instead to rely on the original description of the criminal act charged.

The prosecution also presented an alternative description of the criminal act charged, which stated that when Lahti had returned home in the evening after roughly 11 p.m., the couple had had an argument that had then led to the attack. During the argument, Lahti had jabbed at Auer's chest with a knife causing her a wound that had bled. At some stage, Auer had managed to get the knife away from Lahti and, in turn, used the knife to stab him in the arms and hands, as well as stabbing him twice in the side and once in the armpit. Auer had also hit Lahti twice on the head with a heavy object with fatal results already before the start of the emergency call, and the groaning sounds heard in the background of the call were coming from a previously made recording. According to the prosecution, this meant that Auer could have disguised the murder after the last blows took place and before the emergency call began.

This alternative description of the criminal act charged was no more than partially based on the new presentation of evidence. The description of the criminal act charged was the same as the original, only now it included a reference to the pre-recording of the victim's groaning sounds. The description still considered the starting point of the murder to have been a family argument that got out of control, even if the child had not described this in any way. The premeditation of the act, the involvement of a child in homicide, the use of protective shields made of towels and the presence of satanism in accordance with the new evidence had been completely forgotten from the description of the criminal act charged.

In other words, the prosecution proposed two alternative descriptions of the criminal act in this new round of court proceedings. Either Auer had finished the murder of Lahti during the emergency call and the sounds made by Lahti in the background of the emergency call were authentic or, alternatively, Auer had murdered Lahti before the emergency call and the sounds Lahti made in the background of the call were playing on a recording that had been made earlier.

The Satakunta District Court ruled that Auer was guilty of murder. The District Court made the same conclusion this time as well that there was no outsider present, meaning the only possibility was that Auer was the murderer. The District Court did not consider that the prosecution's claims regarding the premeditation and premade recordings were proven. The suggested use of protective shields covered with brown towels during the homicide remained completely unresolved. All the new evidence, which the prosecution had used to get the Supreme Court to order a whole new round of legal proceedings, seemed to be entirely without relevance, at least in the reasoning of this court judgment.

Then, the Vaasa Court of Appeal dismissed the charge. The Court of Appeal considered that the matters apparent in the emergency call recording did not exclude the possibility of an outside perpetrator with adequate certainty. It did not find the child's account of the use of the cassette player credible and took the view that the claims of the premade recordings were not proven in any other way either. According to the Court of Appeal, the results of the investigation conducted on the crime scene pointed more towards an outside perpetrator than to Auer.

2015. The prosecution now applied for leave to appeal from the Supreme Court for a second time. This time the application was argued by stating that the Court of Appeal had raised the standard of proof unusually high and that this decision by the Court of Appeal deviated from the existing legal praxis. The prosecution also proposed that it was in the interests of the credibility of the legal system to accept this application.

Later, the prosecution delivered further new evidence to the Supreme Court which came from the examination of the emergency call recording by a team of sound professionals. This team consisted of the following people: sound analyst Tuija Niemi, conductor Raine Ampuja, Professor Tapio Lokki, music producer Mikko Raita and composer Otto Romanowski. The team concluded unanimously that part of the sounds in the emergency call recording was indeed pre-recorded and had been played in the background of the emergency call. According to the team, this was proven, among other things, by the fact that Auer had been breathing on the phone but only a fraction of a second later her voice could be heard from the same room as the victim. The distance between the phone and the fireplace room was roughly 10 metres, making it impossible that Auer could have moved there in the given time. In the same manner, although Auer's voice could be heard a moment later from the same room as the victim, after only two seconds she was talking on the phone again, and no sounds of any movement could be heard between these two instances.

Referring to the results of the sound team, the prosecution proposed that Lahti had not been killed during the emergency call as Auer had claimed, but before the call. The sounds made by Lahti, the sounds made by Auer in the vicinity of Lahti while he was alive, and the sounds of the steps all originated from a recording that had been made before the emergency call. The Court of Appeal had questioned why there was no sound relating to Auer moving to the fireplace room and back to the phone at 2:03–2:08 minutes in the recording when sounds from walking on glass and running should be clearly audible. The prosecution stated that the new investigation provided an answer to this: there were not supposed to be any sounds like those because Auer did not visit the fireplace room at this stage and was actually still on the phone, and the sounds assumed to be made by Auer near the victim were actually coming from the premade recording. This description of the criminal act charged corresponded to the previously presented alternative description.

Auer's defence then asked sound designer Micke Nyström to give an expert statement on the emergency call recording and to compare the observations made by Ampuja's team to his own. Nyström gave his statement on 5 November 2015, and his views differed significantly from the views of the other team. According to Nyström, nothing heard in the recording suggested that a separate premade recording had been used in the background of the call in any way.

The Supreme Court did not grant leave to appeal in the case, and the acquittal ruled by the Vaasa Court of Appeal therefore remained in effect.

4. SOUNDS OF THE MURDERER

Why does the murderer not say anything?

Tuija Niemi, sound analyst of the National Bureau of Investigation (NBI) Forensic Laboratory, wondered in each trial why no spoken words from the murderer can be heard on the emergency call recording and why the murderer does not say anything to the victim. According to Niemi, in her experience the killer would have been saying something to the victim – her view on this was based on other emergency calls she had listened where a violent situation and long-lasting fight had been going on in the background. Aside from the Ulvila murder, Niemi could not remember any other cases, except for the emergency calls of the Jokela school shooting, where the perpetrator had not said anything and had instead only killed their victims. Niemi considered the absence of any speech from the killer not only strange but also an indication that no outside killer was present. However, it is likely that the majority of the emergency calls listened to by Niemi were related to so-called 'ordinary' homicides, which are associated with domestic violence or substance abuse.

If the murderer could be clearly heard speaking in the recording, this would be strong proof that an outside perpetrator had been present. However, it is not possible to draw the opposite conclusion equally strongly because there are other natural explanations for the lack of speech. The fact that the murderer cannot be heard speaking cannot be used to draw the conclusion that no outsider was present – it is merely one of many options.

It is also possible that the murderer had said something to the victim even though it cannot be heard on the emergency call recording. According to the media, the Jokela school shooter shouted threats in the school corridors, even though Niemi had not heard him speaking in the emergency calls. In the Ulvila case, the murderer could have spoken to the victim before the emergency call started, or perhaps any speech was not loud enough to carry to the phone or was covered up by other sounds. On the other hand, neither Auer or her eldest child who had been present reported that they had heard the murderer speaking, so perhaps the murderer did indeed not say anything.

The murderer was described as being masked in such a way that their face was not fully visible. Perhaps they had covered their face in order not to be recognised, and perhaps they had been silent for the same reason. The murderer had forced entry into the family's home by breaking the window glass of the back door and was armed with two offensive weapons – the murderer was clearly not coming to talk things through, but to kill. Perhaps they simply did not have anything to say to the victim.

Silence is not especially unusual in untypical homicides. The murderer in the Sello shopping centre in the city of Espoo did not say a word while shooting his victims in 2009, and the attacker in the Savo Vocational College in the city of Kuopio also said nothing when attacking his victims with a longsword in 2019. The attacker in the town of Varkaus did not say anything in 2012, only beginning to stab the victim suddenly. The killer in the city of Kauniainen was silent when she knifed her victim in 2023, and the double killer in the city of Pori had nothing to say to his victims when he shot two sleeping women with a crossbow in 2007. School shooters, other mass murderers and hired killers do not always talk. None of these examples describe a long-lasting violent fight, but they do indicate that those guilty of a homicide do not always speak.

When a person has made the decision to take another's life, they may not feel it necessary to say anything at that point. Silence in particular may be a sign of the premeditation, cold-bloodedness and determination of the perpetrator. Ordinary homicides, where the situation escalates into violence because of an argument and a sudden burst of rage, are a different matter: they typically involve shouting various threats or insults while attacking the other person. Premeditated murders are in a chapter of their own; these murderers are more of a silent kind. The silence may also be a sign of the perpetrator's psychosis or of strong contempt for the victim.

Fighting and swearing

'*Ulvilan tappajan ääni tallentui nauhalle*' ('*Ulvila killer voice recorded on tape*'), was the headline printed in the Ilta-Sanomat newspaper on 8 March 2007 when the police announced that it had a recording of the emergency call in its possession, and that the murderer's voice had been recorded on it.

The emergency call recording was delivered to the NBI Forensic Laboratory for examination soon after the murder. The aim was to clarify the background sounds heard on the recording and use them to find out what had happened during the call. However, the first transcription of the emergency call was made by Senior Detective Constable Matti Mäkinen who was the technical investigator at the beginning of the murder investigation. The primary intention in making

Mäkinen's transcription was to create a rough examination of the information that could be obtained from the call and get its contents quickly available for the use of the police investigation. The transcription included one possible sound made by the perpetrator, and this was described as a grunt. In addition to the sounds from the victim, the transcription included hardly any descriptions of the background sounds, with a few of exceptions: 'tuolin jalan raapaisu lattiaan' ('a scrape of a chair leg on the floor'), 'lähestyvät juoksuaskeleet' ('approaching running steps') and 'kolinaa' ('clatter').

Tuija Niemi, the NBI sound analyst, gave her first statement on the matter on 13 December 2006. According to this statement, you can hear the following during the call: a woman calling the emergency response centre from the house, the victim groaning in the background and, at one point, a small girl talking to the operator. No other person can be heard talking clearly in the background. In some parts, very brief male voices can be heard, but it is impossible to make out whether they come from the victim, the emergency response centre or an outsider in the house. The victim cannot articulate properly any more during the call, which makes it particularly difficult to make out what is being said. The woman is away from the phone between 1:43 and 2:42 minutes on the recording; the girl is on the phone during this time and the woman is presumably near the victim. Groans from the victim, shouts from the woman, sounds of fighting and sometimes running footsteps can be heard in the background. At 2:39, a loud clunk can be clearly heard that could have come from the victim being hit or falling. After this, a fainter clunk can also be heard at 2:41, after which the victim stops making sounds.

According to her transcription, Niemi estimated that sounds made by the perpetrator can be heard at three different moments. The first of these was written as 'Lyöh' and placed at the same timestamp as

Mäkinen's observation describing a grunt. The second sound was written down by Niemi as '(n)ui vaa' and the third was marked as an unclear word with '…', with the comment 'kuulostaa miehen äänellä' ('sounds like a man's voice'). The running steps heard by Niemi correspond to the parts described as 'lähestyvät juoksuaskeleet' ('approaching running steps') and 'kolinaa' ('clatter') in Mäkinen's transcription.

In her transcription in 2006, Niemi had written that several clunks and steps can be heard in the background of the recording as follows:

(Translator's note: in translation the original format has been followed as much as possible. According to Niemi's clarification for her entries in her 2006 transcription, words entered in brackets mean unclear parts or alternative interpretations. The only such case in the below list is at 1:06 where she has entered '(Äihh)', a groaning sound, followed by '(Häivy)' which means 'Get lost'. In other words, Niemi has not been certain what she has heard and has therefore listed two alternatives.)

0:50   [Dragging sound] *movement of a chair, sofa or other similar heavy object, or is the victim moving?*

0:56   [a click] Victim: Öhh/ [a clunk] Victim: Ähh/
        is something hit so hard that it causes clunking sounds or are the sounds coming from the phone line or is the victim moving?

1:06   Victim: (Äihh) (Häivy)
        [A dragging sound] *movement of a chair, sofa or other similar heavy object? could also be the victim's groaning sounds, can't make out.*
        Victim: Äähh, Auuh.

1:48   [a click]

1:55   [rustling, running steps] *are the perpetrator and woman running?*

2:25   [rustling, possible sounds of steps] or something similar

2:27   *in the background sounds of fighting, groans of the victim*

2:39 [a loud clunk] *beating sounds on a door or the floor, or is the victim being hit?*

2:41 [a metallic sound + a faint clunk] *a strange sound further in the background?*

2:46 [a metallic sound] *a strange sound further in the background. similar to the one at 2:41?*

The police then had the emergency call recording examined once again, this time in the Hypermedia Laboratory of the University of Tampere in early 2008. The examination was carried out by Senior Assistant Mika Sihvonen. The resulting transcription was more detailed than the previous ones and contained more sound observations; it also specified the quieter sounds more accurately. Sihvonen had entered possible sounds made by the perpetrator at eight timestamps:

(Translator's note: the original format from Sihvonen's Finnish transcription has been followed as much as possible. Timestamps written into the transcription text by Sihvonen have been removed to avoid repetition. The removed timestamps have been indicated with an em rule [—].)

0:37 [a possible sound made by the perpetrator: Uh]

1:01 [a possible sound made by the perpetrator: Räh,]

1:07 [a possible sound made by the perpetrator: Rreeeihhh…]

1:15 [a possible sound made by the perpetrator: TU!]

1:56 [A sound made by the perpetrator, 'A grunt', —]

2:25 [a-jaa] (heard during a series of steps, either the voice of the victim or the perpetrator)

2:29 (possibly a sound produced by the perpetrator during a hit)

2:38 [a possible sound made by the perpetrator: hä]

Sihvonen had also written down several clunks and footsteps that can be heard in the background of the recording as follows:

0:40   Clunk/step + the victim's voice + a sound resembling the hitting of a wooden lath
0:49   [at least 4 running steps]
0:50   [A sound resembling the dragging of a piece of furniture]
1:06   [a rapid series, possibly steps]
1:09   [movement of a piece of furniture after the first cry of the victim] [a louder clunk before the last cry and possible steps]
1:17   [two: clicks]
       {Translator's note: Sihvonen has most likely meant 'two clicks'}
1:20   [a louder sound resembling a dragging/chafing sound]
1:48   [a possible series of steps]
1:55   [8 steps]
2:07   [a loud thump, followed by screams of the victim]
2:24   [a small clunk (possibly the fall of an object) —]
2:25   [8 fast steps, —] [a louder clunk at the fifth step]
2:29   [A loud clunk, — , after which the voice of the victim cannot be heard on the recording.]
2:39   [A loud clunk, —]
2:42   [Another quieter clunk with a metallic post-echo, —]
2:46   [— possibly a light clunk from the bedroom]

The listed sound observations by Sihvonen were mainly the same as in the transcription made by Niemi, but here the sounds had been described in more detail and there were also more of them. Sihvonen's transcription also had significantly more sounds of footsteps marked down than Niemi's.

So, during the period 2006–2008, the emergency call recording was transcribed three times separately, by Mäkinen, Niemi and Sihvonen in that order. All three had interpreted the grunt heard at 1:55/1:56 minutes as a sound made by an outside perpetrator. The emergency call recording had also been listened to by all the police officers involved in the murder investigation. For more than a couple of years at this time, it seemed clear that in addition to the victim's cries for help, you could hear sounds of fighting and male voices in the background of the emergency call recording. It was considered that these male voices did not match the sounds made by the victim but belonged to a person outside the family.

According to the first investigator in charge, no one in these first two years proposed that there was no outside murderer present or that there were no sounds from them present on the recording. Instead, the belief was that the emergency call showed that the victim was indeed killed by an unknown perpetrator who left the house during the call. However, no clues were obtained from the recording regarding who this outside person was. They were presumed to be male on the basis of eyewitness observations, unfamiliar DNA recovered from the crime scene and the sounds heard in the background of the call recording.

According to Auer, the murderer forced entry into the house, and her child also reported that she had seen an unfamiliar man leaving through the broken window. In addition, forensic investigation by the police also concluded that there had been an outsider present. Did this prior information have any effect on subsequent sound observations made of the emergency call? It is naturally possible, as a lot of unclear and partial sounds or sounds that are difficult to recognise can be heard in the recording. These can be easily interpreted to fit anyone's own presumptions.

The sounds of the murderer disappear

Analyst Tuija Niemi of the National Bureau of Investigation has listened to the emergency call made by Anneli Auer on 1 December 2006 hundreds of times over the years. The analyst has not heard any sounds made by an outside killer from the recording.

The Iltalehti newspaper, 19 May 2011

The police changed the official role of the victim's wife, Anneli Auer, in the crime from injured party to suspected perpetrator in early 2009. The pre-trial investigation report does not indicate the reason why she was now under suspicion. It is known from his own statements to the media and from his book that the new investigator in charge, Pauli Kuusiranta, found that Auer had not originally been sufficiently investigated and that, in order to be able to use coercive measures ordered by a court of justice against her, she now had to be officially made a suspected perpetrator. The police immediately started a covert operation against Auer during the course of which an undercover police officer, Seppo Mäkelä, made contact with Auer and began pretending to be her boyfriend. Auer's home and phone were each monitored and tapped.

In the autumn, the police asked their sound analyst to generate a second statement on the emergency call recording covering, among other things, possible sounds made by an outsider, sounds of fighting, sounds made by a person exiting through the broken window and sounds made when walking on pieces of glass. On 13 August 2009, Niemi gave a statement in which she changed her initial evaluation of the recording radically. According to the new statement, no sounds made by an outsider could be heard in the background of the call. There was no speech from an outsider, no fighting with the victim, no walking on glass and no exiting through the window. Niemi now interpreted the different clattering sounds and other sounds heard in the background as being related to the victim's movements. She now interpreted the victim's groaning to be the result of his injuries and the pain caused by the attempts to move. As for any sounds of walking on glass or exiting through the window, Niemi had not described hearing them this time either.

In summary, in this new transcription there were no markings to indicate sounds made by an outsider. Of the three instances on the recording that Niemi previously presumed to be sounds from the perpetrator, one was now marked with certainty to be a sound from the victim, one was marked as an unknown sound and one had been removed from the transcription altogether. In addition, the new transcription had two instances of speech but the speaker had not been identified. The first instance was 'Mite mä pääse linjoi' ('How do I get on the line') with the accompanying transcriber comment *'This line does not sound as if it was spoken by the woman or the girl, is it coming from the emergency response centre?'*, and the second instance was 'Aja...' (Translator's note: 'aja' is the second-person singular imperative in the active present tense of the Finnish verb 'drive', but it could also be a part of another word.)

It is unusual and contradictory that a human-made sound or speech remains unidentified, or that a previously heard sound goes missing completely from the transcription, while at the same time it is thought definite that no speech or other sound from an outsider can be heard in the recording. It would have been more honest to state that it was not possible to know for certain the source of every sound heard in the recording.

To a very large extent, the new transcription included the same background sounds as the previous one, but the new one was naturally missing the entry *'taustalla kamppailun ääniä'* (*'in the background sounds of fighting'*), and the entry '[metallinen ääni]' ('[a metallic sound]') at 2:46 minutes had been removed completely. The mention of the metallic sound had been left out likely because Auer had already returned to the phone at that point, so there should not have been any background sounds coming from far away when at this stage, according to the police, the victim had already died, and no outsider was supposed to be present. In court, Niemi admitted that she had not marked all the background sounds into her transcription. She explained that she had not written in all thuds because they had only been very faint sounds, nor all groaning because she had interpreted them to come from the victim. This was a rather weak reasoning for the lack of entries. Especially in this situation where guilt was being argued over with particular reference to missing sounds, the sound analyst should have noted down all that was heard in the recording in great detail.

The situation was now completely different from before, as now the emergency caller was being suspected of murder and Niemi's interpretation of the soundscape of the emergency call should have been adapted according to the changed circumstances. Did the changed situation and the new background information obtained from the police have an effect on Niemi's altered evaluation? It strongly seemed that this was the case, but when questioned on it in court, Niemi recounted that the new information had had no effect on her observations; she had based her altered interpretation on the fact that she had now compared the original emergency call recording to sounds recorded in an emergency call reconstruction made by the police, and that for this reason she had now interpreted the sounds heard differently.

To summarise this, the background sounds of the emergency call had remained the same but Niemi's interpretation of them had now changed. In court, Defence Counsel Juha Manner asked Niemi what she thought the sounds were, since the same sounds could still be heard in the recording nevertheless. Niemi could not relate what the same background sounds still audible on the emergency call recording were, stating only that the kind of fighting sounds heard on the police reconstruction recording could not be heard on the original emergency call recording. When Manner then asked Niemi what sounds of fighting are in general, she replied that you could hear grunting, brawling, shouting and the sounds of furniture being moved in the reconstruction recording, and that usually people communicate when they are fighting each other.

In the first round of legal proceedings, Niemi justified her altered interpretation by saying that on hearing the reconstruction of the emergency call recording made by the police, she had found that the sounds caused by the policemen wrestling in the fireplace room – when reconstructing the actual crime – were different to the sounds heard in the background of the real emergency call recording. During the second round of legal proceedings, Niemi also began to justify her altered interpretation by comparing this call with her own past experience in emergency calls where a violent situation is in progress.

The dragging sound heard on the emergency call recording has been described in the transcriptions of Mäkinen, Niemi and Sihvonen as, among other things, 'a scrape of a chair leg on the floor', 'movement of a chair, sofa or other similar heavy object', 'a sound resembling the dragging of a piece of furniture', 'movement of a piece of furniture' and 'a louder sound resembling a dragging/chafing sound'. A similar dragging sound can be heard at several points in the recording (at 0:50, 1:06 and 1:20). The sound has been interpreted fairly consistently as a sound made by a moving piece of furniture by all who have examined the recording. In addition, the crime scene photographs show that the bed in the fireplace room had moved out of its position. On the basis of this sound alone, it is of course not possible to determine who moved the bed or why. However, the sound does appear to have been created in the heat of fighting – the fireplace room is only a small space, and it can be deduced from the blood traces found there that fighting took place on the bed as well as next to it.

In answer to Manner's question in the courtroom about what sounds of fighting are in general, Niemi had referred to the sounds of a moving piece of furniture as an example of sounds heard in the reconstruction made by the police. However, now Niemi interpreted the dragging sound as having come from the victim trying to get up and brace himself on the bed, causing the bed to move, or from the victim lying on the floor and pushing the bed with his foot. Niemi has clearly now based her interpretation of the cause of the sound on the assumption that there was no one other than the victim in the fireplace room at the time. On the basis of the emergency call, one cannot be convinced that there had not been an outsider present because the emergency call proves the opposite or leaves the matter unclear at the very least. It is possible the police have either convinced Niemi that no outsider was present or that it was very important she would give a testimony according to this in any event. The sound is most likely to have come from the movement of the bed, but did the bed move in the heat of the fighting between an outside perpetrator and the victim, or did the victim move the bed alone?

In her transcription in 2006, Niemi had entered she had heard moving sounds of a piece of furniture, a click, clunks, possible sounds of hitting and beating, sounds of fighting and metallic sounds further in the background. Sihvonen had written down that the following could be heard from the fireplace room: sounds of heavy footsteps, several clunks, thumps, sounds of hitting, clicks, moving/dragging/chafing sounds of a piece of furniture, and a clunk with a metallic post-echo. Sound designer Micke Nyström reported in his statement that several indications could be heard in the recording that another person had been in the same room with the victim. Nyström listed in his statement sounds caused by an outside person and other background sounds he had observed from the recording. These are as follows:

0:49.20	Clearly heavy footsteps before a heavy object is briefly moved. Anneli is on the phone. The steps have a regular rhythm and they are determined. A sound, '*öh*', made by a man can be heard between the steps. It sounds like an exertion sound, not like a groan from pain.
0:52	Hitting sound
0:56–0:59	Jukka is hit twice with a hard object
1:01–1:12	Sounds of fighting, several whacks. Before Jukka's last scream, a quickly uttered '...*ttu*' might be just distinguishable before a hard transient sound of a strike (there is a hard change in the sound wave).
1:13–1:36	A completely different male voice clearly says '*vittu*' ('*fuck*'). Also the '*äh*' sound (a grunt) differs from Jukka's voice.
1:54–2:02	Male voice: '*äh*' (a grunt). Belongs clearly to a different vocal register than Jukka's sounds. Anneli runs outside barefoot. The running stops at the opening of a door. The sound of the door opening is similar to the reconstruction sound made by the police, but the door is opened more furiously in the actual recording. It sounds as if the door would go completely open, that is, hit the hinges after the opening sound.
2:41–2:43	A step on glass can be heard.

Can you hear the murderer's voice in the background of the emergency call? Yes, you can. At 1:55–1:56, a clear grunt of the murderer can be heard. This has been heard by Mäkinen, Sihvonen, Hemmi and Nyström. According to Nyström, the vocal register of the person making the grunt is clearly different from the victim's. According to Hemmi, the voice is not the victim's voice, but a voice more resonant and richer in tone. In 2006, Niemi was uncertain whether this same sound was 'Yöh' made by the victim who was retching or 'Lyöh' made by the perpetrator. However, in 2009, Niemi was certain that the sound belonged to the victim and used the marking 'Yöh/ *retching, a grunt*'. (Translator's note: the transcribed sound 'Lyöh' may also refer to some conjugated form of the Finnish verb 'lyödä' [to hit, to strike].)

Sihvonen heard possible sounds made by an outside murderer in a total of eight instances and Nyström in five. Both have stated they heard the murderer swearing. Sihvonen and Nyström also heard the murderer's footsteps from the fireplace room at 0:49–0:50 in the recording when Auer is on the phone. The sounds heard by Niemi, Sihvonen and Nyström at 2:41–2:46 as well as the sounds heard by Niemi and Sihvonen at 3:14–3:16 may also be sounds made by the outside murderer. Auer has already returned to the telephone at 2:42.

It is puzzling to read auditory observations from the experts that differ so much from each other. Some of them have stated that they have heard swearing and other sounds made by an outside person as well as the sound of blows and other sounds indicating fighting, whereas some of the experts have stated that they did not hear any of these. Personally, I can hear the murderer swearing and grunting in the background at a few points in the recording, and it feels difficult to believe that someone else would not hear the same.

On the basis of the emergency call recording, it can be reliably said that some human voices can be heard which cannot be linked with certainty to the voice of any of the family members that were present. In addition, human-made sounds (steps, clunks, thumps, dragging sounds, etc.) can also be heard whose source cannot be confirmed with certainty based on the sound itself. Several sounds that are difficult to recognise can also be heard, and it is therefore impossible to know how these sounds have been created.

In multiple parts of the recording, a sound can be heard that resembles a blow followed by a cry of pain from the victim, and this can be interpreted as a reaction to the violence directed at him. The recording gives the strong impression that a fight is going on further away in the background, but it is not possible to make any certain conclusions based merely on unclear and unidentifiable sounds. The victim's groaning and cries are made in agony, and he repeatedly asks her wife to come and help. It is clear that, at least on the basis of the emergency call recording itself, the possibility of an outside perpetrator cannot be excluded.

5. EMERGENCY CALL RECONSTRUCTIONS

As part of the investigation into the murder, the police carried out a reconstruction of the emergency call in the homicide house on 25 November 2008. The intention was to find out which kinds of sounds become recorded onto the emergency response centre's system when a situation such as the event being described is reconstructed with two persons fighting in the fireplace room. The emergency call scenario was acted out and recorded in its entirety over two versions. In the first, the voices of Auer, her daughter and the victim were acted out in accordance with the transcription with no outside perpetrator. In the second version, where an outside person was thought to be present, a fight was included in the reenactment in the fireplace room in the background of the call in addition to the voices.

The first reconstruction recording of the emergency call, the one without an outside perpetrator, differs from the real emergency call recording because of the silence in its background. Nothing can be heard from the background at all, except for the sounds made by the policeman acting the part of the victim. It may be that he did not move in the fireplace room at all during this, or that his movement did not produce enough sound to cause it to transfer to the phone to be recorded. Nevertheless, it is an undeniable fact that, in contrast, various sounds can be heard in the background of the real emergency call recording. When the first reconstruction recording created is compared to the real one, the difference is evident.

The second reconstruction recording, the version with fighting in the background, resembles the real emergency call recording much more in its background sounds, even if the background sounds of the reconstruction and the real situation are not fully identical. Regarding the fighting, it can be presumed with good reason that the wrestling of two rather evenly matched policemen creates a different kind of fight with slightly different sounds than in a situation where one of the fighters is in possession of an edged weapon and using it with the intent to kill.

The clattering sounds heard from the background of this call reconstruction are also slightly different compared to sounds in the real recording. In the background of the reconstruction, it sounds like someone was kicking pieces of firewood or dropping them on the floor in the fireplace room (the sounds resemble one of the single reconstruction sounds recorded by the police where a single piece of firewood is dropped on a tiled floor). These kinds of sounds are not found in the real emergency call. However, the reconstruction versions do have many similarities with the original recording. For example, the background sounds are covered by sounds from nearer sources in the reconstructions in the same way as in the real emergency call, when a person speaks to the phone from a very short distance or yells into the phone.

One rather amusing detail was that in the reconstruction including the fight with an outside perpetrator, the victim can be heard to make sounds right from the start of the call, whereas in the reconstruction with no outside perpetrator, no victim sounds are actually heard until later, and this is the point where Niemi has entered them in her own transcription. This difference is completely artificial and produced by the police. If this was an attempt to prove that the sounds made by the victim should have been heard in the real fighting situation from the beginning of the emergency call, then this theory from the police has surely also gone down the drain.

Sounds made by the victim have been written down in the transcriptions as follows: Mäkinen at 0:50–2:08, Niemi at 0:23–2:28 and Sihvonen at 0:02–2:28. The transcribers' observations of sounds from the victim are in clear relation to the accuracy they have entered background sounds into their transcriptions. In his transcription, Sihvonen specifies background sounds more widely and precisely and also hears the victim's sounds in the longest time period, whereas Mäkinen has written down the victim's sounds in the shortest time period and his transcription contains very few background sounds. It can be presumed with good reason that sounds made by the victim, even if they are faint ones, can be heard right from the beginning of the call. In the real emergency call, the victim is not silent for the first 23 seconds as presented by the former investigator in charge, Pauli Kuusiranta.

In addition to these entire emergency phone calls, the following different separate sounds were recorded as part of the reconstructions of what happened: sounds made by the victim in different positions in the fireplace room, different running sounds (barefoot, with slippers and with boots), sounds of running water (in the kitchen and bathroom), sounds of various doors opening and closing (front door, eldest child's room, utility room and bathroom), footsteps of the presumed perpetrator for about one metre from the fireplace room to the side of the living room (from an upright position, from a kneeling position on the floor and then from the same positions again but with pieces of glass on the floor), sound of the fireplace door and the sound of a bed sheet chafing against the floor.

The name of one of the sound recordings draws attention: 'Anneli siirtää uhria' ('Anneli moving the victim'). This recording does not contain an actual reconstruction sound at all but instead ends immediately after the introduction 'ensin Anneli siirtää uhria' ('first Anneli moves the victim'). The blood traces at the crime scene did not indicate that the victim would have been moved by anyone – so why was this particular sound reconstruction recording made in the first place and where did the reconstruction sound go?

The police also made separate recordings of reconstructed fighting sounds in the fireplace room. One hard clunk/thump can be heard in the reconstruction recording but no sounds, for example, of a piece of furniture moving. The policeman acting the part of the victim groans and shouts almost constantly, saying: 'Annu tule auttamaan, tule auttamaan, tule tule auttamaan' ('Annu come help me, come help me, come come help me'). Only one or possibly two sounds made by the policeman acting the part of the killer can be heard. No stepping on glass can be heard, but it is not known if glass was on the floor at this time.

In the reconstruction, a range of single sounds were also recorded by the emergency response centre. These were made by dropping different objects on the parquet or tile floors, or in other words the floors in the living room and the fireplace room of the homicide house. According to the introduction to the recordings, these were testing what had caused the metallic clink sound that had carried from the fireplace room's floor. The test objects were defined as a filleting knife, a dental bridge, a camping axe, a piece of firewood, a large piece of glass and a ballpoint pen or similar object, as stated by the police in the reconstruction recordings. A filleting knife, a piece of firewood and a dental bridge were all found on the floor at the crime scene, which makes testing them understandable. The window of the back door had been broken, and that explains the dropping of a large piece of glass for testing. At some stage, a camping axe was suspected to be a possible second instrument of the crime. The relevance of the dropping of a ballpoint pen is not entirely clear, unless it was done to have a comparison when finding out how possible it is to distinguish the sounds caused by different falling objects in a reliable way. All the sounds were recorded clearly onto the emergency response centre's reconstruction recording, which is not really surprising because no additional sounds can be heard at any time around them, not even the breathing of the police officer holding the receiver.

One difference is that the conditions around the reconstruction did not correspond exactly to those of the incident and for this reason, the word 'reconstruction' gives the wrong impression of what the police were doing. It is true that the reconstruction was made in the homicide house using the same landline phone as the real emergency call, and that the call was directed to the same location in the emergency response centre. Even the operator was the same person as was present during the incident, but in terms of the acoustic properties, the conditions of the homicide house did not correspond to those existing at the time of the crime. New residents were living in the house and the furniture and other parts of the interior differed from the ones present at the time of the incident. The house had noticeably fewer items and less textiles, the window glass of the back door was intact, and the back door was closed. According to Niemi's statement, the pieces of glass spread on the floor were fairly large in size, not small fragments like at the actual crime scene.

The forensic investigation report from the police states that the making of the reconstruction sound recording was videoed with two video cameras; the first camera captured events in the fireplace room and the second captured the emergency calls made from the kitchen. Niemi related in the court that she had participated in the reconstruction and that the event had been recorded on video. For some reason, the police did not want to add the videos in question to the trial material and claimed that the reconstruction had not been filmed at all. The video footage could have been used for observing many noteworthy factors in the situation, for example how and where events took place in the house, how and where the policemen were fighting, whether they were fighting on pieces of glass, the position in which the phone receiver was held while the sounds were recorded, whether there was a lot of difference between the soundscape recorded into the video and the one recorded by the emergency response centre, and so on.

On 13 August 2009, the police asked Niemi to compare the reconstruction recording and the original emergency call recording, and Niemi gave her statement on the same day: according to her, no speech or any other sounds made by an outside perpetrator could be heard in the background of the original recording. The sounds of fighting as well as the sounds of walking or running on glass were also missing from the original recording. Similarly missing were the sounds of a possible outside perpetrator leaving through the window of the back door in the fireplace room and other sounds caused as they are leaving (stepping on broken glass and jumping out of the window).

Niemi based her newly altered conclusions on the comparison between the reconstruction recording made by the police and the original emergency call recording. When I listened to the reconstruction recordings myself, I could not help but wonder how and why Niemi ended up presenting the reconstruction in question as the reasoning for her changed interpretations, but I guess she had to validate them with something. Perhaps the entire emergency call reconstruction was made for that particular reason – so that the sound analyst had at least some rational-sounding reason to alter her observations this radically.

Especially perplexing is the reasoning Niemi provided for why she no longer interpreted the fighting sounds heard in the original recording as such after the reconstruction was made. In her commentary to the prosecution on 16 April 2010, Niemi wrote that during the reconstruction the people 'fighting' in the fireplace room (the police officer acting the role of the victim trying to resist the attacking police officer) caused, for example, movement of the furniture which can be heard in the recording. This is the same thing Niemi reported to the court as well. However, these moving furniture sounds can be heard in the original emergency call recording and were also noted down in Niemi's transcription, but after the police reconstruction she did not, for one reason or another, consider them as fighting sounds but instead as sounds from movement of the victim. This interpretation cannot be argued with the reconstruction where the furniture moves when the policemen fight in the fireplace room.

In her commentary, Niemi also wrote that 'both (especially "the victim") made different kinds of sounds compared to those that can be heard during the emergency call; grunting and other kinds of sounds resulting from someone defending themselves could be heard. These are missing from the original emergency call recording'. The fact that the policeman acting the role of the victim is producing different kinds of sounds than the victim in a real situation is not a very reliable basis for making conclusions. The sounds made by the police 'victim' depended on the individual officer himself and how he performed his role. In the reconstruction, the sounds made by the police 'victim' were not spontaneous but acted. The differences in the sounds made already start with the fact that the police 'victim' was not actually stabbed with a knife in the situation, so he did not have the same injuries as the real victim and was not being actually killed.

According to Niemi's statement, the original recording was missing the sounds of someone walking or running on pieces of glass and the sounds of the perpetrator leaving. The sounds of walking or running on broken glass were missing in the reconstruction recordings as well, with the exception of the separately recorded sound described as 'tekijän askeleet' ('steps of the perpetrator') where a single step is heard being made on a piece of glass – this sound was recorded successfully onto the emergency response centre's system, while there are no sounds at all of the perpetrator leaving. At the end of one of the sound files, an introduction saying 'seuraavaksi hyppääminen terassille' ('next, jumping to the decking') can be heard, but the file ends there. The police had apparently recorded jumps from the fireplace room to the decking with the back door open, but this naturally does not correspond to the real situation on any level. It would seem Niemi's conclusions of the missing sounds rested on reconstruction sounds that were produced individually and separately without interference from any others, rather than the recorded sounds of the acted-out murder situation.

The actual probative value of the emergency call reconstruction made by the police was virtually non-existent, but, regardless of this, the sound analyst used it to validate her changed interpretations. According to Risto Hemmi, the recordings made in the reconstruction can provide some indicative information. One sound may resemble another in some ways, but the microphone in a telephone has been optimised to capture sound from close distances and therefore sounds coming from further away are not captured clearly, which makes interpreting them rest somewhat greatly on guesswork and presumptions. The reconstruction had also failed to provide any timeline information, indicated as the first reconstruction call lasted 5 minutes 7 seconds and the second call 5 minutes, whereas the original call was 4 minutes 20 seconds long.

On 2 December 2011, the police again made additional sound recordings by calling from the homicide house to the emergency response centre. This time the following sounds were recorded: various walking and running steps, jumps from the fireplace room to the decking with the back door open, opening and closing sounds of doors (front door, draught lobby, back door, dishwasher, refrigerator, freezer, among others) and shrieks from different distances, as well as the button pressing and winding sounds of three different cassette players. At the same time, Niemi used an artificial head, placed in position with sound equipment attached, to examine which of the sounds could be heard behind the closed bedroom door of the three younger children in the family.

The police sought the assistance of the United States Federal Bureau of Investigation to compare the sounds produced in the reconstruction with the original sounds of the emergency call recording. According to the FBI's examination report, dated 27 April 2012, no definitive scientific conclusions could be made from the original recording because of many acoustic variables, the complicated nature of the recording environment and the limitations presented by the recording system (microphone in telephone handset, telephone transmission system and digital recording system characteristics). The FBI found that the reconstruction sounds from the crime scene were carefully produced with low levels of competing noise and were audible in the recording captured by the emergency response centre. However, comparing the sounds produced in the reconstruction with the original sounds of the emergency call recording did not provide conclusive results.

It is likely that separate minor sounds actually captured by the emergency response centre's system in the reconstruction may have been covered by other sounds because of the different conditions at the time of the murder or may have been so minor in nature that it was impossible to distinguish them in the original recording because of multiple different overlapping sounds (voice spoken into the phone, sounds made by the victim). The caller may also have directed the phone's receiver differently in the real emergency situation compared to the direction used by the police officer in the reconstruction, producing a significant impact on the capturing of the sounds. Even if a sound can be heard on the reconstruction recordings, we cannot reliably conclude that it should definitely be possible to hear it in the original recording.

6. EXPRESSION INDICATING THE INTENT TO KILL

Auer yells 'die'

In the autumn of 2009, it was reported in the news that a sound analysis that had taken hundreds of working hours in the National Bureau of Investigation Forensic Laboratory had produced a chilling result. The sound analyst had managed to dig up a two-syllable word from the tape that could not be heard or recognised by ear alone. Auer says 'u-o-l-e!' on the tape.

This finding, from the emergency call recording in 2009, is unusual in many ways. No one had heard the yell in question made by Auer before. The first investigator in charge, Juha Joutsenlahti, related that he had listened to the emergency call recording at least 300 times and had not heard 'uole' or 'kuole' ('die') during his time as the investigator in charge, and the people examining the recording had not reported hearing them either. Sound analyst Niemi, who made the finding, recounted that she had also listened to the recording several hundred times but had not encountered this word before.

A few months prior to this finding, in the summer of 2009, the police were still uncertain whether it was a woman or child's voice that was heard and what the voice was saying in the part of the recording in question. This is revealed in email messages which were part of the investigation material that was originally concealed and only made part of the trial material because it was demanded by the defence. The email messages show that a sound file entitled '*225661_06_0203_two_speakers*' was delivered to the FBI and that they were asked what the woman or child is saying at 2:03 in the emergency call. The email messages do not contain the FBI's answer to the question but do indicate that on 11 August 2009 a representative of the FBI asked Niemi to make a laboratory visit to Washington and, on 13 August 2009, suggested two alternative dates for this visit in September. It is not known how the exchange of messages continued, but it is known that Niemi never went to Washington. She received an urgent task from the police regarding the emergency call recording on the same day – they wanted to know which word can be heard at 2:03 in the recording and who says it. The question was exactly the same as the one posed to the FBI earlier.

Before the urgent task was given, Detective Sergeant Tapio Santaoja had already stated to Niemi in a phone conversation that he thought that at this point in the recording Auer could be heard to say 'kuole helvetti' (translator's note: these words literally mean 'die' and 'hell' in English respectively, but if used in this manner, 'hell' could be thought of as an expression of frustration). Niemi gave her answer to the police on the same day, stating that the part of the recording in question contained overlapping speech by Auer and the victim. The sounds made by the victim are very indistinct and only sounds containing 'l' and 'a' letters can be heard. Auer says a two-syllable word which has an indistinguishable beginning but the ending most likely features the sounds (u)-o-l-e.

On 21 August 2009, the police asked the forensic laboratory to examine how the caller vocally stresses the word 'u-o-l-e' and what tone the caller uses to swear 'helvetti' ('hell') at 2:07. On 28 August 2009, Niemi provided the following statement about the matter: 'The caller starts the word (u-o-l-e) very high and the pitch descends towards the end. The voice intensity is rather high. The tone is mainly declaratory or commanding. It is difficult to interpret the tone because the victim is also making sounds at the same time'. At the 2:07 point, Niemi stated that she could not hear the caller swearing here (transcription entry: 'Anneli: .../').

It is peculiar that Niemi – who had not heard the word present in the recording before and been uncertain only a few months ago whether the person saying the word was a woman or a child – was now able to describe the word letter by letter, identify that the person speaking was Auer, caller on the emergency conversation, and describe what tone of voice had been used when saying the word. However, the reason why she was not able to make these descriptions much earlier is even more peculiar. The 'kuole' ('die') yell in question can be heard rather loudly and clearly in the emergency call recording used as part of the trial material. Even the prosecution has stated that everyone who has listened to the recording, can hear Auer saying the expression referred to as 'kuole' ('die') at that point. The sound analyst, who could be regarded as a professional in recognising sounds, words and speakers, had not heard the word or at least had not made out what was being said and had not identified the speaker with certainty before the police told her that Auer is saying 'kuole' ('die') at the part in question.

Which is more likely – that the sound analyst had not heard Auer's yell expressing the intent to kill for over two years, even after listening to the emergency call recording hundreds of times, or that the entire 'kuole' ('die') yell could not be heard originally in the recording at all?

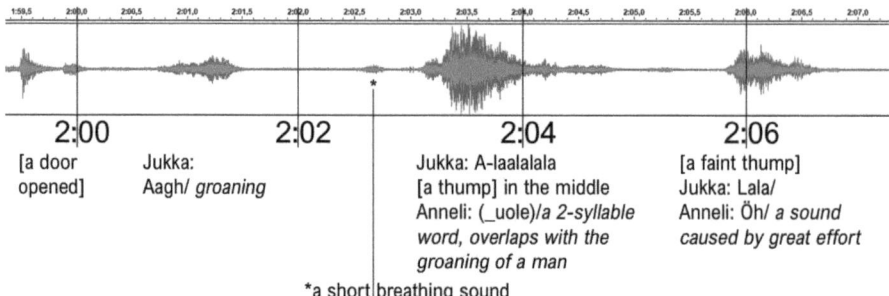

The figure above shows an oscillogram I made of the part in question in the call and the sounds transcribed by Tuija Niemi in 2009. A short sound missing from the transcription has been marked in the image with an asterisk, and this short sound will be discussed later.

The absence of the yell from the original emergency call recording would explain the fact, which seems almost unbelievable, that this yell had gone unnoticed by all of the people who had examined the recording despite having listened to it numerous times. It is not a quiet whisper but a rather strong sound, a yell, that is very audible and can be seen as a large form on the oscillogram. The sound is nearly as strong as voice spoken directly into the phone and clearly stronger than, for example, the victim's cries of pain, which can be heard and seen at the same time as the yell on either side of it and which Niemi had noted in her transcription.

It is noteworthy that Niemi displayed particular caution regarding the interpretation of the word. In court, she related that she could not hear the first letter of the word and was unsure of the second one as well. She could hear the letters o-l-e but was unsure of this too because the sounds made by two people overlap at this part and she could not be certain which sound was made by each person. Why was Niemi this cautious and uncertain about one word while she otherwise related her perceptions strongly and with certainty? Was it because she knew that the entire word was not supposed to be in the recording at all?

Judging from the documents, the yell in question might not have been completely missed after all. The transcription made by Matti Mäkinen already had the entry: 'miehen valitusta ja naisen huutoa. Ei selvyyttä' ('a man groaning and a woman yelling. Indistinguishable'). Based on this, it seems Mäkinen heard that Auer is yelling something but could not make out what it was. In the first transcription made by Niemi in 2006, notation on the same part of the event (2:02) has been written down with 'Nainen' ('Woman') as the speaker and the line/comment as '.../ 2-*tavuinen sana, ei saa selvää, päällekkäin miehen valituksen kanssa*' ('.../ a 2-*syllable word, indistinguishable, overlaps with the groaning of a man*'). From this, it would seem that Niemi too had already heard Auer saying a word at this time. Niemi had even written down the number of syllables but could not make out any more of what was being said at the time. Therefore, on the basis of the documents, it would appear that the yell or unclear word spoken by Auer would have been in the recording originally, but it would have possibly been more difficult to hear because neither of the aforementioned could make out what it was.

A few things cause astonishment, nevertheless. To begin with, Niemi's entry style in the part of the transcription in question differs from that in other areas. In other locations, unclear words have been marked with an ellipsis but without a syllable count, and, on the other hand, some very unclear words have been written down by writing the letters or sounds one after another, that is words that do not have any proper meaning, such as 'pyyjääpää', 'Vittikö', '(n)ui vaa' and 'ännou' exactly as the analyst has heard them. Some words have been entered with two different alternatives, such as 'Yöh' and 'Lyöh'. However, in the part in question, Niemi did not speculate on any of the sounds or letters. Why?

She does not describe the sound as a yell either, even if the transcription includes descriptions of other yells. For example, in two instances, the speaker has been written down as 'Nainen' ('Woman'). In the first instance at 1:54, the line/comment reads 'Mitäkö/ *huutaa raivokkaasti*' ('What/ *yells furiously*'), and in the second instance at 2:22, the line/comment reads 'Hei, lopeta/ *huutaa tekijälle*' ('Hey, stop/ *yells at the perpetrator*'). Another part that draws attention is the entry written directly after the notes on the 2-syllable word at 2:02. The speaker is written down as 'Nainen' ('Woman') and the line/comment as 'Öh/ *voimakkaan ponnistuksen aiheuttama äännähdys, siirtääkö uhria?*' ('Öh/ *a sound caused by great effort, moving the victim?*'). What could make the sound analyst think this when she has referred to an outside perpetrator in several places and written down possible sounds made by an outside perpetrator, sounds of fighting and sounds that suggest the hitting of the victim? Why would she think Auer would move the victim when the alleged perpetrator is present at the house? This would not seem to fit the transcription from 2006, and it makes one think that the transcription is actually not the original from 2006.

It is true that the yell heard at 2:03 sounds like a woman, and it matches Auer's voice. If the voice is heard from the homicide house, it can be concluded that it belongs to Auer because it is known that no other woman was present in the house. However, the Vaasa Court of Appeal considered (in its legally valid judgment in 2015) that there remained a possibility that the person yelling '(u)-o-l-e' is not the accused but another person, or that the accused was not in the fireplace room at least at this stage. The yell resembles the word 'kuole' ('die') a great deal, but there is not an absolute certainty that this is the word in the recording. Personally, I do hear the word 'kuole' ('die') in the recording, even when I have tried to hear some other word that would only resemble this in part.

Auer herself has not denied that the voice is hers, but has said she feels she would be more likely to have yelled, for example, 'älä kuole' ('don't die'). When heard in the trial, Niemi related that she does not hear the word 'älä' ('don't') before the word '(u)-o-l-e' in the recording. However, in her letter to the prosecution on 16 April 2010, Niemi writes the following: '...the word in question is preceded by an "ä" sound produced by Amanda and that the child may be trying to say a word beginning with an "ä" sound, such as "äiti" ('mother') or "älä" ('don't'), because she might be even seeing her mother or father at this point. But, that would mean that both are on the side of the living room or that the child sees the mother, for example, picking up an object and tries to say "älä" ('don't')?' [Translator's note: the question mark at the end of the quote is in Niemi's original text.] With this, Niemi apparently refers to the part marked with the asterisk in the figure of the oscillogram on page 79 (a short breathing sound).

Even if it is not an official statement and Niemi intended her commentary only for the use of the prosecution, the comments show us her way of thinking and what her imagination produces when a concrete auditory observation is not present. Niemi has not written down the mentioned 'ä' sound (or breathing sound) as made by the child in her transcription, but later in 2015, when Niemi became part of conductor Raine Ampuja's team (the group of expert witnesses of the prosecution), she was in agreement with them that the breathing sound does not belong to a child but to Auer and that no 'ä' sound is heard before the word 'kuole' ('die'). Niemi's statements are continuously contradictory, and this matter is no exception. She does not hear Auer saying 'älä' ('don't'), but she can hear the 'ä' sound produced by the child before the word 'kuole' ('die') is spoken. And then years later, Niemi believes that the voice does not belong to the child, but to Auer and there is no longer an 'ä' letter sound present.

Hearing an 'ä' sound spoken by a child in this part of the recording is not, of course, impossible, but it cannot be used alone to make elaborate conclusions of the kind Niemi has made in her commentary letter to the prosecution. From the sound of one letter, it is not possible for anyone, not even a sound analyst, to deduce which word a child was intending to say. According to Micke Nyström, after the breathing sound made by the child, a guttural/nasal sound or rasp can be heard with the sound of inhalation, and Nyström describes this as the breathing of a child swallowing their tears. The breathing sound is suddenly cut off in the recording here for some reason. It is completely possible that Niemi is correct in that the child starts to say something but her voice is cut off and covered up beneath Auer's 'kuole' ('die') yell.

This part of the emergency call is significant because the police used it in their attempts to get Auer to confess. The police claimed it indicated Auer's intent to kill and that it proved Auer had killed her husband. In the police interviews they referred repeatedly to this part of the call and to the fact that there was nobody from outside the family in the house. According to the police, this had been verified from the emergency call recording.

The police also reported that the two eldest children told them that their parents had been fighting, although in fact neither of them had spoken of this. On the contrary, when asked, the children had denied hearing their parents fighting on the night of the homicide. The police also said the children had told them there had been no outsider present, even though the daughter had said in every hearing that she had seen the perpetrator leaving through the broken window and the son had not seen anybody because he had been in the room of the other three children the whole time. The police also implied that the eldest daughter would have known the whole time that her mother was the murderer.

In addition to this, the police reported that according to the police dog handler no one had left the plot of the building (occupied by the building and its land), although in reality the plot and its front boundary could not even be examined with the dog because the paramedics and police had walked around both the plot and the house. The dog was led on the outside of the plot along its side and back boundaries. In the dog handler's view, nobody had recently walked over these boundaries, but someone might have walked around in front of the house. The dog picked up a scent trail from one of the furthest away corners on the back of a neighbouring plot, and from there the dog turned and moved along a lawn strip to the Tähtisentie street and only lost the trail after it reached an area of asphalt. According to the dog handler, in the weather conditions prevailing on the night of the murder, the trail of a person may remain on a lawn for three to four hours but would already disappear from asphalt within 30 minutes. From this it can be said with certainty that someone had walked along the lawn strip near the homicide house during the night at around the time of the murder.

Quotations from Anneli Auer's police interviews:

'You have told us that you ran away from the perpetrator barefoot. According to the sound analyst, the person running away was wearing shoes. You have told us that the perpetrator had been stabbing Jukka. According to the statement on sounds in the recording, no sounds of stabbing can be heard, nor any sounds made by an outside person. You have told us the perpetrator left through the window. According to the dog handler, no one has left your plot.'

'The police have found in their own investigations that during the time of the crime there were no other people in the house besides you, Jukka and the children. This has

also been verified from the recording of the emergency response centre relating to your call there on the night of 1 December 2006. Your daughter and son have told us that there were no other people in the house in addition to their mother and father.'

'With certainty, there were no other people in the house besides you, Jukka and your children. You say the word mentioned previously (referring to the part "u-ole" in the emergency call at 2:03) and, a few seconds after this word mentioned previously, the sounds made by Jukka stop. This is when Jukka is killed for certain. How do you explain this?'

'Your daughter and son have heard you and Jukka arguing loudly during the night.'

'Do you not think that there is a huge contradiction between the sound analyses, the accounts of your children and your own previous accounts?'

'You are aware that your daughter was also awake during the time the crime occurred and that she heard and partially saw you and Jukka arguing and yelling loudly. Additionally, your daughter was on the phone when you were alone with Jukka in your bedroom and, during that time, you uttered the two-syllable word "(u)-o-l-e". Jukka died during that time and your daughter is aware of this. What kind of thoughts does this provoke in you, the mother of a small child, when you consider the events from the perspective of your daughter?'

'There is overlapping speech between you and Jukka at 2:03 in the voice sample. At this point, you said a two-syllable word whose sounds at the latter part are most likely "(u)-o-l-e". This word is uttered during a time period where you are off the phone for 59 seconds and during which Jukka is killed. According to the statement of the National Bureau of Investigation, no sounds made by an outsider can be heard from the bedroom. At that time, you were with Jukka in the bedroom. There was no one else in the house according to your children and the sound recording. Given these facts, do you consider it likely that you have killed Jukka Lahti?'

The child asks, 'Who is there?'

The case gets even more peculiar when another fact is learned – that Mika Sihvonen, senior assistant in the Hypermedia Laboratory, University of Tampere, did not hear Auer yelling at all in the part in question, but heard something totally different than what can be heard today in the version that is considered the official recording. Here Sihvonen has noted in his transcription that a child quietly asks the question, 'ketä siellä on?' ('who is there?'). How was it possible to confuse the one-word yell 'kuole' ('die') made by a woman with the three-word interrogative clause 'ketä siellä on?' ('who is there?') posed by a child with a quiet voice?

Perhaps this deviation in observation does not make matters peculiar, but it explains everything. No one heard Auer's yell in the recording during the first years following the murder, but after 2009 everyone can hear it. It might still be credible that the exact elements of the yell would have been unclear, but when an observation differs this significantly from others, this seems impossible. The observations made by Sihvonen regarding the majority of the emergency call are very similar to those made by Niemi, but in this particular sound they differ considerably. Sihvonen is completely alone in this observation – no one else has been able to hear the said part in this way or, at least, there are no records of this happening.

Confusing the voice of a woman with the voice of a child can presumably be possible up to a point, as analysis on the matter was requested from the FBI as late as June 2009 (regarding what the woman or child is saying in the part of the recording in question). Then, during the trials, no one proposed any longer that here the voice belonged to a child. Even if the voice of Auer and a child could be confused – which I would personally consider quite unlikely – it is not possible to confuse a yell with a quiet voice. Distinguishing quiet and loud sounds is probably the easiest part of audio examination because in addition to auditory perception, the difference can be perceived easily by examining the sound in a visual representation. The tone of the yell has been described as declaratory or commanding, and this is another matter that does not fit an interrogative clause. The difference between these two alternatives is so significant that it cannot merely be about disparity in interpretation.

Could it be a mistake caused by inattention, a human error, or something else? I asked Sihvonen himself if he could have been mistaken. He could not explain why no other examination of the recording had reached a conclusion that agreed with his own interpretation but did consider that the possibility of making a mistake spanning multiple words was unlikely. Sihvonen recounted that he had checked the content description several times and had also gone through the draft at the final stage of the work again by listening to the recording, observing the audio in a visual representation and comparing these with the text together with a detective. Sihvonen also said that he would without question have made corrections if the visual representation had shown, for example, any noises at all, let alone speech, which he had not yet written details of in his draft.

It is therefore difficult to explain the difference in interpretations of this part of the recording as a mistake. It is not possible to confuse Auer's yell 'kuole' ('die') with the child's question 'ketä siellä on?' ('who is there?'), either as an auditory observation or as a visual observation. On the basis of to the rest of the transcription, Sihvonen's work was accurate and thorough, so it also cannot be deemed likely that he would have purposefully made up an observation in this particular part.

One other difference in the transcriptions is that Sihvonen's entries are missing the 'Öh' sound at 2:06 which Niemi (2006, 2009) describes as a sound caused by great effort. This sound is quite loud and easy to hear, just like the previously mentioned 'uole', making it curious that it is missing from an otherwise detailed transcription. In the end, it must be questioned whether Sihvonen was listening to a different recording from the one included in the trial material. This seems the only possible explanation, but at the same time it would mean that the emergency call recording in the trial material would not fully correspond to the original emergency call. The part that is different from the original is located at 2:00–2:08 in the recording.

The different interpretations of part 2:00–2:08 in the emergency call (bold added by author):

(Translator's note: in translation the original format has been followed as much as possible for the transcriptions of Niemi and Sihvonen. The full transcriptions of Mäkinen and Ampuja's team were not available during translation. In the below list, to separate the translations from the transcription text, spoken lines are first in Finnish, followed by translation into English between vertical bars.)

Mäkinen 2006	(man) AAH! (a man groaning and **a woman yelling**. Indistinguishable) Woman: Tuleeks sielt kettään? | Is anyone coming? |
Niemi 2006	Victim: Aagh/ *groaning* Victim: A-laalalala/ lala/ *cannot speak clearly anymore* **Woman: …/ a 2-syllable word, indistinguishable**, *overlaps with the groaning of a man* **Woman: Öh**/ *a sound caused by great effort, moving the victim?* Woman: Tuleeksielt kettää | Is anyone coming | / *comes to speak near the phone*

89

Sihvonen **2008**	[Victim: O-Aauu!] Woman: [Gives a sob on the phone] [Victim: Aauuaa-aaa!] **[Daughter: Ketä siellä on? |Who is there?|]** [a loud thump, followed by screams of the victim] [Victim: Aa!] [Victim: Aa!] Woman: Tuleek siält kettään? |Is anyone coming?|
Niemi **2009**	Jukka: Aagh/ *groaning* Jukka: A-laalalala/ *cannot speak clearly anymore* [a thump] in the middle **Anneli: (_uole)**/*a 2-syllable word, overlaps with the groaning of a man* [a faint thump] Jukka: Lala/ **Anneli: Öh**/ *a sound caused by great effort* Anneli: …/ Anneli: [faint steps] Tuleeksielt kettää/ |Is anyone coming/|
Ampuja's team **2015**	victim's groaning sound a woman's breathing sound victim's groaning sound and **woman: Kuole! |Die!|** victim's groaning sound and **woman: _o-__u** woman makes a sound, starts talking to the phone from a very close distance

At 2:01, all the people examining the recording have heard the victim's groaning sound. After this Ampuja's team has noted that they hear Auer's breathing sound and Sihvonen has noted in his transcription that

he hears Auer's sob, but Nyström has noted at the same point that he believes it is a breathing sound made by the child. Niemi has not written down a breathing sound here in either of her transcriptions, but in court she evaluated the sound as one made by a child. When Niemi later became part of Ampuja's team, she then agreed unanimously with the rest of the team that the breathing sound was produced by Auer. In principle, the breathing sound can belong either to Auer or the child because the child is on the phone at the time in any case, and Auer could also have been very close to the phone at that moment.

Everyone believes that after this moment the victim is heard groaning, but at 2:03 where Mäkinen notes 'a woman yelling', there is confusion. According to Niemi's 2006 transcription, she hears Auer saying a two-syllable word, whereas in June 2009 she hears an unclear word spoken by Auer or the child, and then, on 13 August 2009, she hears '_uole' spoken by Auer. Ampuja's team, which Niemi is by then also part of, hears Auer saying 'kuole' ('die') at this point in 2015. Differing from all of these, Sihvonen hears something totally different and reports hearing the daughter asking 'ketä siellä on?' ('who is there?'). No one after the year 2009 hears the child's question at this point in the call. Instead, those examining are rather close to being unanimous that Auer says 'kuole' ('die') or at least something very similar to it.

It seems impossible that while doing his analysis Sihvonen would have listened to a recording with the same content as the one later added to the trial material. This is because, in the recording used in the trial, the '(_uole)' found by Niemi on 13 August 2009 is clearly audible even to anyone without any training or experience in the sound industry and because it is impossible to confuse '(_uole)' with the three-word question 'ketä siellä on?' ('who is there?'). The sound made here can be seen as a large form in the visual representation of the sound, which both Niemi and Sihvonen have examined carefully on their own while going through the recording. Even Raine Ampuja was still wondering this matter in 2012 while behind a pseudonym at a crime-related web forum, as follows: 'JL huutaa jälleen, mutta nyt spektriin sotkeutuu AA:n KUOLE, jota tutkija ei alunperin kuullut lainkaan, vaikka se olisi Spektriäkin tutkimalla ollut ilimiselvää!' ('JL cries again, but now the spectrum is mixed up with AA's KUOLE [DIE], which the analyst did not hear originally at all, even though it would have been obvious just by examining the spectrum!')

By comparing these statements, it can be concluded with quite a strong probability that the emergency call recording no longer corresponds to what was originally audible in it. The change can be heard at the very least at 2:02–2:07 minutes. It most likely starts at the point where the sound following the breathing sound made by Auer or the child is cut off strangely, and it ends a little before 2:08, which everyone hears in the same way as Auer posing the question 'Tuleeks sielt kettään?' ('Is anyone coming?'). The exact format of the transcription of this question has been written down slightly differently between the transcribers, most likely depending on how they have interpreted the dialect, but the meaning of the question is exactly the same. Sihvonen has not noted any sounds made by Auer between 2:02–2:07 in his transcription, while during this time Niemi hears Auer saying 'uole', 'öh' and something else that is indistinguishable. In the same time frame, Ampuja's team hears, or sees from the visual representation of the sound, Auer saying the words 'kuole' ('die') and 'o(pp)u'. According to Nyström, new audio layers and interference noise can be heard clearly in this period. Lahti's groaning sound also has an unusual double echo which cannot be heard in any other part of the recording. Nyström also considers that the so-called 'o(pp)u' word speculated by Ampuja's team sounds synthetic, and this kind of synthesis does not happen in any other part of the recording.

Are the interference noises related to movements around the phone's receiver being handled and the compressing recording system, as Nyström is guessing, or are they signs of manipulation of the recording? Was the same kind of treatment applied to the emergency call as was applied to the photograph appendix supplied with the pre-trial investigation report, where a photograph that revealed mistakes was replaced with another one that was more accommodating of the police?

On the basis of all of the above, it strongly seems that the emergency call recording has indeed been modified from the original to better suit the intentions of the police. The changing of the recording must have taken place between 2008 and 2009, the changes themselves relating to the recording timed at 2:03–2:07 minutes. It is noteworthy that this is exactly the part that the police asked sound analyst Niemi to examine, in rather a hurry, in the autumn of 2009, and it is here where the question 'ketä siellä on?' ('who is there?') was heard previously. This question, posed by the child most likely to her mother, was a direct reference to the fact that the child knew there was an outsider present but did not know who it was. The modifying of the recording killed two birds with one stone – it removed the child's question referring to an outsider and replaced it with a cruel yell that indicated Auer's guilt as she told her husband to die.

7. A LIVE OR PRE-RECORDED MURDER?

The critical 59 seconds

Auer was away from the phone in the middle of the emergency call for a little under a minute, approximately 57–59 seconds. The pre-trial material of the murder had included a timeline of the emergency call indicating the following times: the start of the phone call, the time when Auer left the phone, Auer saying '_uole', the last time the victim's voice was heard, the time at which Auer returned to the phone, the point when Auer says 'nyt hiljeni' ('now it's silent'), and the time of the end of the phone call. The police attempted to prove Auer's guilt with this timeline, pointing out that Auer was away from the phone during the time when Lahti stopped making sound altogether on the emergency call recording. What did Auer do during the time she was away from the phone? Can the emergency call recording provide clarity on this question?

The emergency response centre operator asks Auer to wait when she leaves the phone for a while, using the words 'odota hetki, mä meen hetkeks pois linjoilta, älä sulje puhelinta, älä mee pois' ('wait a moment, I'll go off the line for a moment, don't hang up, don't go away'). Auer responds to the operator by saying 'En' ('No, I won't'). Auer keeps shouting on the phone 'Nopeesti!' ('Quickly!') and 'Kuuleksä ku mun mieheni huutaa?' ('Can you hear my husband screaming?'), but there is no one on the line. Every now and then Auer is shouting and apparently asking her husband if the intruder has left, for example by saying 'Menik... lähtiks se mies jo?' ('Did the man go—leave?'). Lahti's grunting, cries of pain and requests for help can be heard from the background, for example: 'Annuuu, tule tule tänne Annuu' ('Annuuu, come come here Annuu'). Now and then Auer questions down the phone if the help is coming: 'Onks joku tulossa jo?' ('Is someone coming already?').

When the operator has been off the line for nearly a minute, Auer decides to go and see the fireplace room and asks her child to take the phone for the duration. Auer says: 'Hei, mun täytyy ny... Amanda! Tuuksä tänne puhelimeen, mä meen kattoo tonne.' ('Hey, I have to now... Amanda! Can you come to the phone, I'm gonna go look there.'). Auer hands the phone's receiver to the child and tells her that she has called the police and that they've asked her to stay on the line. Auer says: 'Mä soitan poliisil, siel pyydettii et... me pysytään sen linjoil' ('I've called the police, they've asked that... we stay on the line') [the four last words in Finnish are how both I, the author, and Risto Hemmi have heard them in the recording]. The latter sentence sounds as if spoken when Auer has turned away from the phone or already moved slightly further from it. Auer left the phone at 1:46 minutes into the call.

The sounds that can be heard at 1:47–2:42 in the recording when Auer is away from the phone are as follows:

(Italics added by author for emphasis.)

1:48   Lahti: '*No lähe auttaan, Annuu!*' ('*Oh, come and help, Annuu!*')

              According to Sihvonen, a possible series of steps can be heard at this part. It can be presumed that the steps belong to Auer when she is going towards the fireplace room.

1:51   Auer: '*Lähtikse jo?*' ('*Did he leave already?*')

Auer is most likely approaching the fireplace room and asks Lahti on the way if the perpetrator has left. On the basis of this question, she cannot see into the fireplace room at this point.

1:52   Lahti: '*Tule auttaan!*' ('*Come and help me!*')

1:54   Auer: '*Mitä sä [–]!*' ('*What're you [–]!*')

Apparently, she sees the perpetrator attacking her husband at this point.

1:55   The perpetrator: '*Äh*'

Here a possible grunt made by the perpetrator can be heard as he starts coming towards Auer. This has been considered the voice of the perpetrator by Mäkinen, Niemi (2006), Sihvonen, Hemmi and Nyström.

1:56   Auer: '*Vittikö!*' (no actual meaning) Auer sounds startled.

1:58   In this part, Mäkinen, Niemi (2006, 2009), Sihvonen, Ampuja's team and Nyström have all heard Auer's running steps when she runs across the living room to the draught lobby and then outside.

(Translator's note: for this particular timestamp, the entries below are presented as closely as possible to the format in the transcriptions that have been available when translating.)

Mäkinen: 'approaching running steps'

Niemi (2006): [rustling, running steps] *are the perpetrator and woman running?*

Niemi (2009): [running steps] [door opened]

Sihvonen: [8 steps]

Ampuja's team: in the beginning, two to three step sounds approaching the microphone. After that two step sounds are closest to the microphone, after which step sounds move away from the microphone. After the nearest steps, four more step sounds can be heard, of which the first one on a hard floor, the second one on a soft surface (possibly a carpet) and with this a sharp clunk can be heard simultaneously. Two last ones on a hard surface. The two last steps are louder because the movement stops. In this part, the running sounds of one person can be heard. The runner is wearing shoes the whole time.

Nyström: Anneli runs outside barefoot. The running stops at the opening of a door. The sound of the door opening is similar to the reconstruction made by the police, but the door is opened more furiously in the actual recording. It sounds as if the door would go completely open, that is, hit the hinges after the opening sound.

2:01   Lahti: '*Aagh!*'

2:02   Auer: '*Nyyh*' (a sobbing sound)

Auer has come back inside and is breathing near the phone. Would she have already made it next to the phone from outside? The distance from the front door to the phone is not great, so it is possible. According to Nyström, the breathing sound belongs to the child on the phone. This is also what Niemi still thought in 2010.

2:03   Lahti: '*A-laalalala lala*'

Auer: '_uole!' Auer's voice sounds like it is coming from somewhere further.

According to Niemi, in this instance Auer's voice comes from the same distance away from the phone as the sounds made by the victim when taking into account the volume of these sounds.

According to Professor Tapio Lokki from the Department of Media Technology, Aalto University, the victim's groaning sounds and the word '*kuole*' ('*die*') have the same kind of echo, which is why they sound like they are coming from the same room. When they are compared with the voice spoken into the phone's receiver, a clear difference can be noticed between the sounds recorded near the receiver and the sounds recorded from further away.

Music producer Mikko Raita finds that, on the basis of the sound resonance, it can be said that the above sounds – the victim's groaning and '*kuole*' ('*die*') – have been made in the same room, that is in the same acoustic space, and fairly far from the phone.

According to composer Otto Romanowski, the groaning sounds made by the victim, the yell '*kuole*' ('*die*') and the following unclear word have the same spatial echo and dynamics and have therefore taken place in the same space. Depending on the amount and quality of the echo, they have been produced in the space where the victim was present.

It is unclear where Auer is at this point, the voice does not sound like it is coming from next to the phone, but further away. According to Ampuja's team, the sound is carried from the fireplace room.

2:05   Lahti: '*Lala*'

2:06   Auer: '*Öh*'. The sound comes from somewhere further away. The same unclarity applies to this part as to the earlier '*_uole*' part.

2:08   Auer: '*Tuleek sielt kettää?*' ('*Is anyone coming?*') Auer is speaking near the phone.

2:10   Child: '*Hei, onksiäl joku, tulkaa äkkii, mun iskä voi huonosti*' ('*Hey, is anyone there, come quickly, my dad is not feeling well*').

2:14   According to Nyström, sounds of barefoot steps can be heard here when Anneli leaves the phone and goes to another room.

2:16   Child: '*Tulkaa äkkii!*' ('*Come quickly!*')

2:17   Lahti: '*Aa! Kylmää!*' ('*Aa! Cold!*')

2:18   Child: '*Iih!*' ('*Eek!*')

2:19   Child: '*Eii! Iskä, älä kuole!*' ('*Noo! Dad, don't die!*')

2:22   Lahti: '*Aii*'

2:23   Auer: '*Hei, lopeta!*' ('*Hey, stop!*') Auer is yelling somewhere further away, probably at the boundary between the living room and the fireplace room.

2:25   Lahti: '*Ajaa*'

Auer apparently runs away from the entrance of the fireplace room. Niemi has written down an entry of steps in this part. According to Sihvonen, eight fast steps can be heard and a louder clunk at the fifth step.

2:26   Emergency response centre: *'Joo, haloo'* (*'Yes, hello'*) The emergency response centre is back on the line.

2:27   Lahti: *'Se jäi'* (*'It stayed'*). This is the final time the victim makes sounds in the recording. [Translator's note: this could also mean 'he/she stayed' because *'se'* is often used colloquially in Finnish to refer to people.]

Child: *'Nii, tulkaa äkkii, mun iskä voi huonosti, jooko?'* (*'Yes, come quickly, my dad is not feeling well, could you?'*)

In this part, Niemi (2006) has made the following entry: *in the background sounds of fighting, groans of the victim*

2:31   Emergency response centre: *'Joo, sinne on apu jo tulossa. Osaakko sä, onks siel joku aikuinen paikalla nytte'* (*'Yes, help is on the way. Can you... is there an adult present now?'*)

2:35   Child: *'Äiti'* (*'Mom'*)

2:36   Emergency response centre: *'Voisko äiti puhuu?'* (*'Could mom speak?'*)

2:38   Child: *'Äiti tuu, nyt siel puhutaa taas'* (*'Mom, come, now they're talking again'*) [a loud clunk]

Judging from the child's voice, the mother is somewhere nearby, at least within sight.

2:41   [a metallic sound + a faint clunk]

2:42   Auer returns to the phone: *'Mä yritän auttaa, onks sielt tulossa joku'* (*'I'm trying to help, is someone coming from there?'*).

Auer has recounted that she twice went to look in the fireplace room from the side of the living room during the emergency call. According to her, the perpetrator had then come after her or at least turned towards her threateningly on both occasions; she had thought the perpetrator had come after her when she fled, but both times he had then returned immediately to continue the attack on Lahti. Auer described more about her visit to the fireplace room in the emergency call: '…mä juoksin äske ulos, jos mä meen sinne, se lähtee juoksee mun perää. Se meni takas ja se aikoo tappaa mun mieheni, se oli äske viel hengis.' ('…I ran outside a moment ago, if I go there, he's gonna come and run after me. He went back and he's gonna kill my husband, he was still alive a moment ago.').

The sounds heard in the emergency call recording fit the course of events described by Auer. Her two visits into the living room to the edge of the fireplace room can be heard in the recording. During her first visit, it is possible to hear Auer's steps as she moves towards the fireplace room, her yelling 'Mitä sä!' ('What're you [–]!)' at the perpetrator, and then yelling 'Vittikö' after becoming startled. Her running all the way outside and, finally, the door slamming can also be heard. After she has returned inside and come nearer to the phone again, the sound of breathing can be heard followed by her question: 'Tuleek sielt kettää?' ('Is anyone coming?').

From her second visit into the living room, it is possible to hear Auer's footsteps moving towards the fireplace room and her yelling at the perpetrator 'Hei, lopeta!' ('Hey, stop!'), after which another series of footsteps running away are audible. Lahti can still be heard making sounds after Auer's second visit. A very short period of about 10 seconds exists after Auer's second visit during which it cannot be deduced on the basis of the sounds heard where she has been, because neither her speech nor the sound of her footsteps is audible. Nevertheless, she is most likely closer to the phone than the fireplace room because no sounds of moving can be heard in any direction. It is clear that the child has her in sight at the latest at 2:38 minutes in, as we hear her speaking to her mother and asking her to come to the phone.

During the interviews, the police suggested to Auer that '...your daughter was on the phone when you were alone with Jukka in your bedroom and, during that time, you uttered the two-syllable word "(u)-o-l-e"". Jukka died during that time...'. The police claimed Auer was in the fireplace room when she said 'kuole' ('die'). However, on the basis of the sounds in the emergency call recording, Auer cannot be placed in the fireplace room at that time because only a moment earlier she had run across the living room to the draught lobby and then gone outside. No sounds can be heard in the recording that would suggest Auer moved from the front door to the fireplace room via the living room and then back next to the phone. The moving sounds cannot have been obscured by any speech being spoken on the phone either, because the emergency response centre operator was not on the line and the child present was quiet. Therefore, by listening to the recording, it remains unclear where Auer was at the time when she says 'kuole' ('die').

The prosecution proposed the same conclusion as the police – that Auer goes to finish off the murder when she moves away from the phone. According to the prosecution, Auer then hits Lahti on the head with some heavy object and after this returns to the phone. In the recording, it is audible to a listener when Auer makes two visits presumably to the edge of the living room towards the fireplace room, but even if she had gone all the way to the fireplace room, it can still be heard that she returns from there straight away because of the sound of running. During these visits, she would not have had time to do anything. The murder could not have taken place during either visit because Lahti was still making sounds after both occasions when Auer had run away.

Arguments against the prosecution's conclusions include the point that no sounds can be heard of a possible third visit by Auer to the living room, or of any moving off in any direction. Their conclusion is also contradicted by the fact that no blood trails were found on the route from the fireplace room to the phone. The blows with a heavy object directed at Lahti's head caused a lot of blood to fly around and the perpetrator must have been hit with splashes of it. Auer too should have been bloodstained if she had been hitting Lahti mortally on the head. The behaviour of the child on the phone does not suggest that these kinds of events took place. No sounds of walking on glass can be heard in the recording either. At least according to sound analyst Niemi, these sounds should be audible on the recording if someone had walked into the fireplace room.

Jukka Alihanka, Doctor of Medicine and Surgery, conducted a respiration rate analysis on the basis of the emergency call recording and found that before Auer had left the phone her respiration rate was 9 breaths per 15 seconds, or 36 breaths per minute, which is considered a high but natural rate considering the kind of situation at hand. When Auer returned to the phone, her respiration rate was 32 breaths per minute; in other words, the rate had dropped a little. According to Alihanka, the physical activity proposed by the prosecution's version of events could not be performed without a considerable rise in respiration rate. On the basis of the rate measured from the call recording it appeared that Auer had not performed any significant physical exertion during the time she had been away from the phone.

Judging from all of the above, it is not likely that Auer would have murdered her husband during the emergency call. The soundscape of the emergency call recording does not support this claim in any way, but instead proves that the claims of the police and the prosecution are actually impossible.

Premade recording

A retrial of the murder was ordered in 2012 after the prosecution had presented new evidence to the Supreme Court in the previous year, stating that the emergency call recording contained pre-recorded sounds. The idea of the premade recording first arose from the account of one of Auer's children and was seized upon desperately by the prosecution.

Sound analyst Niemi was again asked to provide a statement and now found it possible that part of the sounds heard in the background of the emergency call originated from a recording that had been made in advance. Niemi based her view on the fact that sounds of the victim heard in the background were sometimes loud and so could possibly be coming from a place closer to the phone than they would if coming from the fireplace room where the victim was killed. At other times, the victim's cries were fainter. Niemi considered that there were only two possible explanations for the difference in volume: either the victim had been moving outside of the fireplace room or recordings, which had been made in advance from different distances from the phone, had been playing in the background during the call.

Auer's all cassette players, dictation machine and cassette tapes, as well as all the sound files from her computer, were then examined in the NBI's forensic laboratory but provided no support for the premade recording theory. No sounds of buttons on any cassette players being pressed were heard in the emergency call recording, and no background sounds for the emergency call were found on any of the cassette tapes or the computer's sound files.

The premade recording theory was an attempt to solve the previously mentioned problems, such as why there are no sounds of Auer moving to the fireplace room and returning from there, and why there are no sounds of walking on glass if Auer herself visits the fireplace room. If some of the sounds heard had been pre-recorded and were played in the background of the emergency call, then the fact that the sounds in the emergency call recording did not match with the description of the criminal act given by the prosecution would not matter. The premade recording could explain all such contradictions because any of the unmatched sounds could come from a premade recording played in the background. In this version of what happened, Auer would naturally have had a little bit more to stage than otherwise, but there would have been correspondingly more time for this staging because the murder could have been completed in advance of the emergency call.

The premade recording claim resolved part of the lack of logic in matching the description of the criminal act given by the prosecution and the sounds of the emergency call recording, but it fitted poorly to the idea of a family argument that got out of control. The FBI found no signs of use of a premade recording in the emergency call recording itself. Hemmi also found no signs of a premade recording and, according to him, it would not have been possible to play such loud background sounds as heard in the recording, for example the sound of the bed moving, from the cassette player's speakers. The premade recording theory was, all in all, an idea rather rich in imagination and already an unlikely alternative to start with.

The premade recording theory proved unsuccessful in court, but, nonetheless, the prosecution attempted to present even more evidence of it in support of their application for leave to appeal in the Supreme Court. This time, help was offered by conductor Raine Ampuja, who had contacted the prosecution and told them of his own investigations into the emergency call recording. The prosecution assembled an entire team to examine the problematic part of the emergency call recording at 1:57–2:08 minutes into the file, where Auer's running footsteps, a breathing sound on the phone and the yell of 'kuole' ('die') can be heard. In addition to Ampuja, the team also consisted of sound analyst Tuija Niemi, professor Tapio Lokki, composer Otto Romanowski and music producer Mikko Raita.

This team issued their own expert statement in the matter on 24 September 2015 and concluded that Lahti was not killed during the emergency call but was already dead before it took place. The sounds made by Lahti, the sounds made by Auer in the vicinity of the victim while he was alive, and the sounds of the footsteps all originated from a recording that had been made before the call. The long-lasting violence committed on the victim with a knife could not be heard in the emergency call recording at all. The following stage of the events, when the victim was groaning and mortal hits were directed at his head, had also been played from a recording in the background of the call. According to the team, the words 'kuole' ('die') and '_o(pp)u' (= 'öh') were both said with a particular kind of tempo and intention that proved they were both spoken by the same person. The victim's groaning sounds and Auer's words were spoken in the same room. According to Romanowski, originally according to the police interview notes, the intonation (the commanding stress separating the syllables) and the rhythm of the command word 'kuole' ('die') indicated that the word was a separately uttered intense exhortation. Before and after the yell in question, a thump could be heard, and after the yell, the victim's voice was also heard; this would fit with the events as it would be his reaction to the blow that struck him.

It was clear that one of the team's members, Tapio Lokki, had understood the problem with the lack of logic in the soundscape of the recording. It was difficult to position Auer in the fireplace room at the point when she is yelling 'kuole' ('die'). The problem was that, on the basis of the sounds in the emergency call recording, Auer had actually run further away from the fireplace room just a moment earlier. Lokki resolved this matter by reversing the direction of Auer's running steps, thinking that this way the situation would continue logically. According to Lokki's new version of these events, Auer would have run from the draught lobby to the fireplace room and, a moment later, the victim's groaning and Auer's yell of 'kuole' ('die') would be heard in the fireplace room. However, this presupposed that the situation had been recorded in advance before the emergency call and was played simultaneously with the emergency call. In this case, the recording device would need to have been located somewhere in the living room to make the sounds present to the listener the same way as on the emergency call recording. Romanowski agreed with this new version of what happened, while Mikko Raita was not completely sure of it. The opinions of Ampuja and Niemi on the matter did not transpire from the interviews.

Lokki and Romanowski had attempted to solve the prosecution's problem and position Auer in the fireplace room to yell 'kuole' ('die') and murder her husband. They were correct in that it would have been much more logical if Auer had run towards the fireplace room rather than away from it. To reverse the direction of the footsteps in the course of events, use of a premade recording was required. Lokki and Romanowski tried to make the soundscape work logically in relation to Auer being the murderer but, at the same time, lost the logic of the bigger picture.

Thinking about this, how logical would it be to record the sounds of a murder and then play them again in the background of an emergency call? On one hand, it was suggested that Auer was intelligent enough to stage a live murder in the background of an emergency call by playing sounds recorded in advance. But, on the other hand, she was also supposedly stupid enough to record her own yelling of the word 'kuole' ('die') and play that in the background as well. Why would she not stay carefully on the phone throughout the pretended live murder to gain an alibi for the time the murder occurred? Why would she make things this complicated when she could have simply called the emergency response centre without any premade recordings and say: 'There was a killer here just now, come quickly!'

According to Ampuja's team, Auer's voice (the breathing sound) can be heard on the phone and then, just a fraction of a second later, her voice (as 'kuole' ['die'] is yelled) can be heard from the fireplace room. The distance between these locations is 10 metres, which makes it impossible that she would have had time to move from one place to the other in the said time. Auer's voice saying 'o(pp)u' / 'öh' can be heard again from the fireplace room and then, after two seconds, on the phone again ('Tuleek sielt kettää?' ['Is anyone coming']), without any sounds of movement heard in between. Ampuja's team may be correct about the sounds being made by Auer. But if these sounds can be heard from two places almost at the same time, as the team proposes, how can it be explained?

Ampuja's team considered that the only possible explanation for this is that Auer's yell of 'kuole' ('die') had been recorded in advance and that it was played in the background of the emergency call, but is this really the only possible explanation? Of course not. There is another more probable explanation. The yell of 'kuole' ('die') made by Auer was actually recorded afterwards and was not added to the emergency call recording until later – this makes the soundscape of the emergency call logical.

8. EXIT OF THE MURDERER

Stepping on glass or a technical failure?

The murderer, in the version of events where an external attacker was thought to have been present, was believed to have left the house during the emergency call. It has been concluded that, while exiting, they would have stepped on the chest next to the back door (there was a bloody shoe print on the trousers that were on the chest), leaned an arm on the wall above the chest next to the door (the wall had a bloody wipe mark) and stepped on the lower edge of the broken window in the door and from there, either directly or via the plastic chair outside, passed through to the decking (where there were a few bloody shoe prints as well).

It is unclear at exactly which stage the perpetrator left the house, but it is reasonable to assume that at the very earliest they had left immediately after hitting Lahti on the head. According to the medical examiner, Lahti's head injuries had likely caused him an immediate death, and they had been created only a few minutes before the first patrol arrived at the scene. This was deduced by comparing photographs taken by the first patrol and others taken by the forensic examiners – from these it could be concluded that the pool of blood next to the victim's head had expanded after the first photographs were made.

With rather a strong probability, it can be assumed that Lahti died during the emergency call at 2:28–3:10 minutes into the recording, because after

2:28 no clear sounds made by Lahti can be heard. However, Auer does not say 'nyt hiljeni' ('now it's silent') until 3:11, meaning that she cannot hear Lahti's voice any more. In addition, the perpetrator has most likely left the house before 3:39 minutes into the recording when Auer asks her daughter 'Amanda oliks se viel siel?' ('Amanda, was he still there?'), to which Amanda replies 'Ei, se lähti' ('No, he's gone'). [Translator's note: literally, Auer says 'Amanda, was it still there?' and Amanda replies ('No, it's gone'). 'Se' ('it') is often used colloquially in Finnish to refer to people.] This means a sound made by the perpetrator leaving may possibly be heard in some part of the recording at 2:29–3:39 minutes.

No such clear sounds can be heard in the emergency call recording which connect with certainty to the perpetrator leaving through the broken window in the back door. One can imagine what these kinds of clear leaving sounds would be like and whether those should be audible in the recording. When Niemi spoke in court, she felt that the recording should have had the sounds of the perpetrator leaving – that is, stepping on glass and jumping onto the decking – if an outside perpetrator had been present in the house.

In the second sound reconstruction made by the police on 2 December 2011, jumps were made from the window opening in the back door to the decking and the sound created from the jumping was captured on the recording of the emergency response centre. In the reconstruction, sounds were produced separately without any competing sounds, meaning it cannot be concluded with certainty that the jumping sound should have been audible in the recording of the real situation. The FBI found that the sounds of the reconstruction recordings of the police were carefully produced, they had few competing noises and the sounds were audible, but comparing these reconstruction sounds with the original sounds of the emergency call recording did not provide decisive results.

At 2:29 minutes into the recording, Sihvonen has written down '[A loud clunk … after which the voice of the victim cannot be heard in the recording.]' and Niemi (2006) has noted 'in the background sounds of fighting, groans of the victim'. Even if Lahti's voice cannot be heard after the clunk at 2:29, more clunks can still be heard before Auer says that it has become silent. At 2:39, Sihvonen has described '[A loud clunk…]', and Niemi has commented 'beating sounds on a door or the floor, or is the victim being hit?' in 2006 while she has noted '[a clunk]' for this timestamp in 2009. At 2:42, Sihvonen has described '[Another quieter clunk with a metallic post-echo…]', and, at 2:41, Niemi (2006) has written down '[a metallic sound + a faint clunk]' with the comment 'a strange sound further in the background?'. At 2:46, Sihvonen has entered '[…possibly a light clunk from the bedroom]' and Niemi (2006) has noted '[a metallic sound]' with the comment 'a strange sound further in the background…'. The clunks may be related to the violence being committed to the victim or they may be related to the perpetrator leaving the house.

Sounds can still be heard in the background even after Auer returns to the phone. No certainty has been achieved on the origin and cause of the sounds. After returning to the phone, Auer speaks at a rather loud volume and her voice is close to the receiver, which is the reason why not all of the background sounds may necessarily have been recorded at this stage of the call. Auer and the emergency response centre operator talk almost non-stop until Auer states that 'nyt hiljeni' ('now it's silent'), to which the operator responds with 'sun mies hiljeni vai?' ('did your husband go silent, or?'). After this, a child's shriek can be heard at 3:14–3:16 followed by 'a click'. In the beginning of the murder investigation, the police suspected this clicking sound was the result of the perpetrator dropping a knife on the floor while leaving, or of the perpetrator breaking a piece of glass by stepping on the edge of the broken window in the back door while leaving. At first, Niemi had not heard this sound at all, but this was because she had cut the child's shriek out of her work version and the click sound had been cut out at the same time. Sihvonen had written down 'Tytär kirkuu ja luultavasi [sic] lämäyttää [sic] käsillään' ('The daughter screams and probably slaps with her hands') in his transcription.

According to Risto Hemmi, the sound is a high-frequency crack (around 4 kHz), which could indicate it has come from glass and could perhaps be the result of stepping on broken glass or of the breaking of another piece of glass. The frequency is right at the upper limit of the frequency responses of the phone and the recording system. The origin of the sound is difficult to determine, but the sound it resembles most can be found among the set of single reconstructed sounds made by the police ('soitto 11 *"tekijän askeleet"* ['call 11 *"steps of the perpetrator"*']) where a large piece of glass is stepped on, most likely breaking it in half.

The police asked both Niemi (sound analyst of the National Bureau of Investigation, NBI) and the FBI for a statement about what the click sound is in the recording. According to Niemi's statement on 2 February 2012, the sound could have been produced by the caller (i.e. Auer), it could have come from the background at the caller's end, or it could originate from the recording system itself. The FBI gave the following response in its report of examination on 27 April 2012: 'The "click" which occurs at 3:14-15 has the characteristics of an electronic event (brevity and lack of decay). Typical acoustic events have decay times that are characteristic of the environment. The origin of the "click" was not determined.' Pertti Virtanen, who was in charge of the emergency centre system during the time of the crime, related in his hearing that he did not consider the sound in question an electrical interference and that he was unaware of any such interference found in other recordings from the emergency response centre.

Two versions of the emergency call recording

Is the click in question the sound of the perpetrator breaking a piece of glass while leaving through the broken window in the back door, or is it interference noise from the technical devices, or could it be something totally different? Whatever the case, the click sound caused confusion when it was noticed that two different versions of the emergency call existed which were both claimed to be the original. One of them has the click sound, and the other does not.

In the Court of Appeal in 2014, Niemi recounted that the emergency response centre's system was examined in relation to the click sound to find out how it was possible that there were two different versions of the emergency call recording which were both supposed to be the original. As part of this process, the emergency call was restored twice from the backup recording of the emergency response centre of the Satakunta region in 2012 (on 24 February and 27 March) and the police asked the sound analyst to then compare these restored sound files with the recording provided initially by the emergency response centre.

The following is an excerpt from Niemi's statement:

Investigated samples:

Sample 26 is an audio file named 'p33412_-011206_tahtisenkatu_C9.aud'. It is in the .aud format of the NiceLog system and was obtained from the emergency response centre on 1 December 2006.

Sample 101 contains two recordings, the first of which was copied from a backup recording of emergency calls to the Satakunta region emergency response centre on 24 February 2012 and named '01122006_-klo_024321_ORG.wav'. The second recording was restored from the archive of the same system on 27 March 2012 and named 'p30651_AUD_tahtisentie_01122006-_org_1F.aud'.

(Note: in 2006, backup recordings were on audiotape and one tape contained multiple emergency call recordings. Nowadays digital files are used.)

The matter is unusual because the original emergency call copies should naturally be identical, but also because the dates given in Niemi's statement cause astonishment. According to this statement, the examination request of the police was dated 8 March 2012 and it asks to compare sample 26 with sample 101. According to the statement, sample 101 was received on 16 March 2012 – but is said to contain a file that was not restored from the emergency response centre until 27 March 2012. So, it would seem that the police asked Niemi to compare two named samples on 8 March even though one of them (sample 101) did not exist in its entirety until the 27th, and Niemi still supposedly received this very sample on 16 March 2012. Of course, this may be a writing error or some similar kind of mistake.

In her statement on 11 April 2012, Niemi finds that the files restored from the emergency response centre's system early in 2012 are similar in their content but differ in two ways. The sound of one file is softer than the other, and the click sound already described can be heard in the first at 3:14 minutes in but not in the second. Niemi assumes in her statement that the reason for the difference in the recordings could be that if, during the restoring, the sound file is being listened to and the Automatic Gain Control (AGC) is on, this suppresses the sound in general and this would prevent the recording of the click sound. Niemi's statement is based on guesswork. The matter was not clarified with the people who performed the restoration of the files, which means it is not known if the sound files were listened to as they were being restored, and if they were listened to, it is not known if AGC was on or not.

When being heard in the Court of Appeal in 2014, Niemi also gets confused herself with these different interferences that are allegedly technical. She recounted that she sought clarification about this matter from the Finnish importer of the NiceLog recording system. According to Niemi, the importer told her that if a recording was being listened to while it was being copied from the system, a click sound could have come from the recording system itself. If a copy was made without listening, this would not happen. According to Niemi, the click did not originate from the homicide house but was a sound related to the restoring of the recording (a so-called technical problem). However, this evaluation was completely opposite to Niemi's thinking in her 11 April 2012 statement where it says the click sound specifically disappears during the restoring process, instead of being created in it.

In addition to the above, two strange claims are related to the click sound heard after the child's shriek. To begin with, the sound is claimed to be caused by a technical interference but then it is also claimed that it disappeared because of some technical interference. The technical interference explanation is used as a reason why the sound can be heard and also why it cannot. When the sound is audible, it is assumed to be some interference noise caused by the emergency response centre recording system. When the sound is inaudible, it is assumed to be caused by some aspect of the file restoring process of the emergency response centre's system. Whatever the truth of this, the only important matter seemed to be that the sound in question did not come from the homicide house, and therefore it could not be a sound related to a perpetrator leaving.

To complicate matters further, the click sound also disappears when the recording is filtered. This is what happened to Risto Hemmi when he made his own filtered version of the emergency call. One possible explanation for the click going missing is that the recording has been filtered or manipulated in some way, either during the recording phase or after it. The filtering cannot have been done by the emergency response centre's system itself because the click was audible in the original emergency call recording, first delivered from the emergency response centre on 1 December 2006. No reliable system-derived explanation has been provided for the differences of these files.

I asked the emergency response centre a few years ago if they still had the original Ulvila murder emergency call. In reply I was told that according to the Act on Emergency Response Centre Operations (692/2010) any data was to be deleted from the data system of the emergency response centre when it was no longer necessary for the purpose of use of its register, and no later than five years from the date of the emergency call. I was also informed that all recordings are deleted from the system by the time the five-year time limit defined in the act has passed. My enquiry was then transferred to the National Police Board of Finland because for data kept by the police the data registrar is the National Police Board. The response of the National Police Board referred to the same section of the Act above and explained that the recording had been deleted from the data system of the emergency response centre in accordance with the rules of deletion under the Act.

The emergency call was received on 1 December 2006, and the five-year time limit was therefore 1 December 2011. The response of both the emergency response centre and the National Police Board related that the law had been observed, and the emergency call had been properly disposed of within the time limit. The matter seemed clear, the provision was unequivocal and the responses from the authorities conforming, but, nevertheless, the matter contradicted what I had found in the trial material.

I then also checked the matter with Taito Vainio, the Director General of the Emergency Response Centre Agency. He also replied to say that the emergency response centre had deleted the original emergency call recording within the five-year time limit in accordance with the Act, that is no later than 1 December 2011, and that the emergency response centre had delivered copies of the emergency call to the police only on 1 December 2006. According to Vainio, all emergency call recordings should then be copies of the recordings that were once given to the police, so these would naturally be copies themselves but would be completely identical in their data content to that of the original audiotape recording.

On the basis of this information, the examination requested by the police appears strange, because restoring the Ulvila emergency call from the emergency response centre was no longer possible in reality in 2012. In addition, the deletion of the original recording also means the police could not have given restored copies of the original emergency call to the sound analyst for examination, even if this was what was claimed to have happened. What recordings then did the police ask to compare and why?

It is a fact that the material used in the pre-trial investigation and trials contained two different versions of the emergency call recording.

Version 1 of the recording has the following filenames:

- *'Ulvila_Tähtisent_011206_klo_0243.wav'* (attachment 15 A)
- *'p33412_011206_tahtisenkatu_C9.aud'* (sample 26)
- *'p30651_AUD_tahtisentie_01122006_org_1F.aud'* (attachment 33)

This version has a duration of 4:20.12 and a file size of 4,161,932 bytes. This version has the audible 'click' after the child's shriek. The recording has a two-second-long silent part, containing only white noise.

Version 2 of the recording has the following filenames:

- *'Call1_.wav'* (the file that was examined by the FBI in 2009, *'direct copy of the original evidence'*)
- *'01122006_klo_024321_ORG.wav'* (attachment 32)

This version is almost completely identical with version 1, but it has a slightly shorter duration of 4:20.00 and a smaller file size of 4,160,044 bytes. This version is completely missing the 'click' after the child's shriek – it cannot be heard, and it cannot be seen when examining the sound as a waveform. The graphical representation shows that the two-second-long silent part is completely empty, and on this recording does not contain even noise.

Both of these versions cannot be exact copies of the original emergency call recording because they are not entirely identical. In fact, there is reason to question whether either of them is identical to the real original emergency call either. It is unlikely. This is demonstrated by the unusual passion the police have had in relation to this aspect of case. It seemed to be astonishingly important for the police to prove two things. First of all, the click had to be a noise caused by technical interference – under no circumstances could it have originated from the homicide house, so that it could not possibly represent a sound of an outside perpetrator leaving. Secondly, the police wanted to prove that the emergency call recording from the trial material was definitely real and was identical in content to the original version captured in the emergency response centre.

The police stated that during the further investigations which took place early in 2012 the emergency call was copied twice from the backup recording containing the original call to the Satakunta emergency response centre. However, according to the emergency response centre it had already deleted the backup recording before this within the five-year time limit as prescribed by law, and it delivered copies of the emergency call to the police only once back on 1 December 2006.

To summarise, the authenticity of the emergency call recording was called into question in 2012 because it was discovered that two versions of the recording existed – these differed from each other but both were supposed to be copies of the original emergency call. The emergency call was the most important piece of evidence in the murder case, so it was in the interests of the police to prove the authenticity of the recording. Did the police carry out these restoration tasks as presented and restore a copy of the emergency call from a backup held by the emergency response centre, or was there actually no restoration at all and only stories about it described on paper?

In accordance with law, the emergency response centre must delete emergency call recordings within the five-year time limit, but in 2012, the time limit had already expired. Did the emergency response centre act in accordance with law and delete the original recording within the time limit, or did it merely claim that this was done? Whose interests were greater in the matter? Definitely the interests of the police. And which are more likely to be true – the statements regarding the further examinations carried out by the police or the response from the emergency response centre?

9. BEHAVIOUR OF THE EMERGENCY CALLER

Apparently atypical behaviour

During the pre-trial investigation of the murder, expert statements had been requested from two psychologists, Pirkko Lahti and Lasse Nurmi. The subject of the statements was Auer's behaviour during the emergency call and in the video of Auer's police interview, filmed in hospital on the day after the homicide. The prosecution used the statements as evidence in the court with the subject 'Havainnot Anneli Auerin käyttäytymisestä ja toiminnasta teon jälkeen viittaavat hänen syyllisyyteensä' ('Observations of the behaviour and actions of Anneli Auer after the act suggest her guilt').

Both statements questioned Auer's calmness in the interview video filmed on the day following the murder. Neither of the psychologists considered Auer's calm behaviour normal after a crime this serious and deemed it atypical behaviour.

However, studies on people who have experienced trauma has shown that the range of trauma reactions is wide, and it is difficult to discern a 'typical' emotional reaction. According to psychiatric literature, a typical behaviour of a person in a post-traumatic state of shock is specifically a confusing calmness, in contradiction to what is indicated by Pirkko Lahti and Lasse Nurmi in their statements.

On 7 August 2009, Pirkko Lahti wrote the following in her statement regarding the emergency call:

The emergency call does not display the mother's worry about her children's condition in any way. When there was a killer in the house, a common reaction for a mother would have been to take her children out to safety. In this case, the mother catches the attention of one of the children by shouting to them to come and help her and then sends the child to see if the man has already left. This is something a mother would not normally do because mothers primarily protect their children. Auer does not seem to be worried about the escape and survival of her children at all. Was it really that obvious that the target was her spouse? I think Auer does not show any concern over the condition of her children, but instead places one of them in a situation where they are exposed to danger. The emergency call recording gives me the feeling that Auer is bouncing back and forth, which is of course understandable in an emergency but also creates other impressions.

Lasse Nurmi gave the following statement on 17 August 2009:

As the events progress, I am also astonished by the behaviour of the mother of small children in obvious mortal danger. Why did Auer not protect her children or evacuate them to a neighbour. (sic) *Auer puts her nine-year-old child on the phone to talk to the emergency response centre operator and goes somewhere else during this time. Why? Did Auer assume that the intruder would not do anything to the children? On the other hand, the emergency call does give the impression of people who are very shocked and alarmed.*

Both Pirkko Lahti and Lasse Nurmi were wondering why Auer did not protect her children, and they considered Auer's behaviour atypical. However, they did not express what their perception of this as atypical behaviour was based on, or how common or rare this kind of behaviour might be for someone whose close relative is in a life-threatening emergency situation – or how common this kind of behaviour might be for a guilty rather than an innocent person.

According to Doctor of Psychology Katarina Finnilä-Tuohimaa, called as a defence witness, the statements of Lahti and Nurmi were not expert statements because they contained mainly subjective opinions, speculation and open questions as well as insinuations and communication 'between the lines'. There were no clear conclusions in the statements, and they did not present the information on which the conclusions were based in a manner that would allow an outside reader to understand how those conclusions could be applied in the case in question.

According to Finnilä-Tuohimaa, the subjectivity of the statements was indicated by the strong stands used that were based on mere impressions. The phrases [as used in the original Finnish statements] 'mielestäni' ('I think'), 'tulee tunne' ('gives me the feeling') and 'tulee vaikutelma' ('give the impression') reflect that matters cannot be evaluated objectively, instead it becomes about everyone's own interpretation and opinion, regardless of whether the person evaluating is an expert or not.

Many matters that were addressed in the statements were relevant only if one already considered Auer to be guilty. When both alternatives were considered – that Auer could be guilty or not guilty – the addressed matters were not relevant at all. Contradictions in the statements suggested a preconception of guilt, because no matter how Auer behaved, it always indicated that something suspicious was occurring according to the person issuing the statement. If Auer behaved in an illogical and irrational manner, it was suspicious, but if she was too rational and too calm, then that was suspicious as well. A way of thinking where two contradicting matters both point to the same end result has no scientific basis.

Why, then, did professionals in psychology fall into this unprofessional way of acting? Perhaps the police had convinced them of Auer's guilt, and they wanted to help and gratify the police. There was no scientific research relating to how mothers guilty of homicide behave towards their children in a violent situation threatening the life of a close relative, compared to the behaviour of innocent mothers in a similar situation, and this meant the experts had to give their statements without any such information – therefore these statements had absolutely zero probative value. Experts who conduct themselves in a professional manner would have stated that no conclusions could be drawn about the mother's possible guilt on the basis of her behaviour towards her children during the emergency call, because there is no researched information on the matter. Even poor presentation of evidence can influence the opinions of people, including judges, and therefore this kind of presentation of evidence is not completely insignificant either.

In the trials, sound analyst Niemi had also wondered at Auer's behaviour during the emergency call when it appeared that she was not worried about the safety of her child at all. However, Niemi also did not have any concrete evidence to support her opinion, and in addition as a phonetician she would not even have the expertise necessary to evaluate behaviour on the basis of her training.

The Vaasa Court of Appeal also deemed the emergency call confusing and stated that on the other hand Auer's anxiety could be heard in it, as she was repeatedly asking for help and hoping it arrived quickly. They also concluded that sounds made by Jukka Lahti and the actions and sounds of the child did not suggest that Auer had acted in a violent manner in the situation. On the other hand, Auer's actions were deemed surprising because she did not seem to fear for her own or the children's safety, even though she reported that she was in a situation where an outside perpetrator was trying to kill her husband.

The fact, that Auer does not seem to be afraid for herself or her children during the emergency call points to something suspicious, possibly guilt, according to Pirkko Lahti, Lasse Nurmi and Tuija Niemi. They imply that perhaps Auer knew that there was no outsider present, or that she knew the perpetrator and was aware that they would not do anything to the children. This is one alternative, but there are other possible explanations. In retrospect, Auer's behaviour might not have been logical, well-thought-out or sensible in all respects, but she was dealing with a very surprising and exceptional event – other people may have behaved differently in a situation like this.

It is possible that, as stated by the Vaasa Court of Appeal, Auer was behaving in a manner typical of her, rationalising a stressful event and reacting to it. In that moment, the killer was attacking Jukka Lahti and he was in immediate mortal danger; he needed help. At that point, the killer had directed no threat of violence towards the children and had directed violence at Auer only when she had attempted to interfere in the attack. Roosa Rentola, a Master of Arts who has studied the emergency call, considers it possible that Auer's attention was so heavily focused on the attack happening at that moment to Jukka Lahti that she was simply not able to also pay attention to the children during the call.

I asked Edward Primeau, an experienced American audio forensics expert, to examine the authenticity of the emergency call. He replied with the following: 'The recording is not in English but during critical listening, I believe the persons were true to their emotional state. In other words, it sounds real to me, not actors or fake. It's not English but I have heard a lot of emotional calls and recordings over 37 years so I can disclose that opinion to you.' Primeau does not speak Finnish and cannot therefore take a stand on the content of the discussion but only to the feeling that is conveyed in the speakers' voices. According to him, the emotional states of the people heard in the call are real, not acted.

Nevertheless, the opinions of the various psychologists, sound analysts and judges about the emergency call are based only on the kind of feeling they get from it, and those are their own opinions. Some have more experience on emergency calls and others on human behaviour, but despite this none of them can have definite information through their experiences on how a guilty or innocent person behaves. Only on the basis of scientific fact can probability-based evaluations be made of how common a particular type of behaviour in a particular kind of situation would be with respect to the guilt or innocence of a person.

What does scientific research have to say?

Is it possible to evaluate on the basis of the emergency call whether the call is real and whether the caller is guilty or innocent of murder?

The authenticity of the emergency call can be examined by studying its contents and the discussion between the emergency response centre operator and the caller. Pekka Santtila, Professor, Doctor of Psychology, examined Auer's behaviour during the emergency call at the request of the defence and in accordance with a model developed in the United States. The model was based on the only study that existed at the time on caller behaviour during emergency calls relating to homicides and deaths: 'Analyzing 911 Homicide Calls for Indicators of Guilt or Innocence: An Exploratory Analysis' (2009) by Tracy Harpster, Susan Adams and John Jarvis. This study included a total of 100 analysed emergency calls in which it was known that the caller was innocent in half of the cases and was guilty, or a party to a criminal act in some way, in the other half. The study showed that certain behavioural characteristics were clearly more common in emergency calls for the guilty callers than for the innocent. On the basis of the study, an evaluation form had been created which could be used to determine whether a call had characteristics indicating the guilt or innocence of the caller. No single characteristic is considered proof of guilt or innocence, but instead, because of the nature of the study method, the results are evaluated as probabilities.

Santtila used the form to make an evaluation and ended up with the conclusion that Auer's behaviour during the emergency call did not indicate guilt. Auer asked for immediate help for the victim and hurried up the arrival of the help multiple times, and the call did not include unnecessary or contradictory information or characteristics suggesting the approval of the death of the spouse. The conclusion of the evaluation inclined completely to the opposite direction compared to the conclusions in the statements of Pirkko Lahti and Lasse Nurmi.

The American study was later expanded by some extent, and now the evaluation form in use is based on a study with 200 analysed emergency calls, where the caller was innocent in half of the cases and guilty or a party to a criminal act in the other half. With the help of this method, Master of Arts Roosa Rentola has evaluated Auer's guilt/innocence on the basis of the emergency call in her book 'Kielestä kiinni'. In the book, Rentola goes through the parts of the method in detail and comments after each part on Auer's behaviour in the situation but does not make an evaluation of the whole. Nevertheless, hardly any single part in the evaluation suggests that Auer would be guilty, so I gather that Rentola's conclusion is the same as the one made by Santtila, that Auer's behaviour during the emergency call does not point towards her guilt.

In the book 'Analyzing 911 Homicide Calls: Practical Aspects and Applications' Tracy Harpster and Susan Adams present the Considering Offender Probability in Statements (COPS) Scale they have created. According to the method, the first matter to observe is who the call is about. An innocent caller usually focuses on the victim, does not approve their death or wants to help the victim. An innocent caller asks for help immediately whereas a guilty caller may explain about the emergency but does not necessarily ask for help because they know that help is no longer needed, or they have no motive to get the help to arrive.

Immediately, at the beginning of the call, Auer asks for help and hurries up the arrival of the help multiple times. She relates that her husband is being stabbed with a knife. Then she relates that she has also been stabbed and she is bleeding, but after this, she does not speak about her own condition any more during the call. The call's focus is on Jukka Lahti, not Auer herself. Auer does not say at any point in the call that Lahti has died.

The second matter to observe is what the call is about. An innocent caller is cooperative, provides sufficient information to get help to the scene, describes different details with sensory perceptions, answers questions and takes action that hastens the arrival of help. A guilty caller may explain events unclearly and provide misleading or irrelevant information which is of no use for helping the victim and may even delay the arrival of help.

Immediately, in the beginning of the call, Auer explains about the killer, provides the address and then relates that the victim is her husband and he is being attacked with a knife. She describes the condition of Lahti first and only then her own. The following quotes are from Niemi's 2006 transcription unless otherwise stated. Auer pays attention to the sounds Lahti is making during the call by saying 'Kuuleksä ku mun mieheni huutaa' ('Can you hear my husband screaming') and '...huus äske apua, nyt hiljeni' ('...cried out for help a moment ago, now it's silent'). Auer does not describe Lahti's injuries or bleeding, but because she is in a different room, she might not necessarily have other perceptions of his injuries except for auditory perceptions that are carried to the phone as well. Auer is cooperative, answers questions and gives a coherent picture of the events.

In the beginning of the call, the emergency response centre operator asks 'Kuka siel hakkaa puukolla' ('Who is stabbing with the knife there'), to which Auer replies only 'Heti' ('Immediately'). The operator repeats the question and then also asks 'tunneksä sitä' ('do you know them') and it is not until this third question that Auer answers. When making his analysis, Santtila was uncertain whether this should have been interpreted as not wanting to answer, but, on the basis of the emergency call, he found it was not completely clear if Auer had heard the question or not. Rentola contemplated the same thing – was it about unwillingness to answer the question or did Auer not hear the question or was she focusing on something else at that moment. The victim can be heard groaning in the background at this point.

The third matter to observe is how the call is made. An alarmed, innocent caller may make sounds already before the operator has actually had the chance to answer the phone or speak over the operator in the beginning of the call. An innocent caller is in a hurry and may shout at the operator to speed up the arrival of help. Delaying and passivity may suggest the guiltiness of the caller. The caller may perhaps wish the victim would die or may have already killed them. An innocent caller often stays near the victim when making the call if only possible. Keeping an obvious distance to the victim during the call suggests the caller is guilty.

Auer's breathing sounds can be heard in the beginning of the call already before the operator has said 'Hätäkeskus' ('Emergency response centre'). Auer starts the call by shouting: 'Tääl o joku tappaja/Tulkaa nopeesti/' ('There's a killer here/Come quickly/'). When the operator is asking which locality is in question, Auer shouts over her the following: 'Joku tuli ikkunast sisää' ('Someone came in through the window'). Auer asks for help immediately in her first sentence with 'Tulkaa nopeesti' ('Come quickly') and hurries up the help four times during the call by saying

'Heti' ('Now'), 'Hei nopeesti' ('Hey quickly'), 'Nopeesti' ('Quickly') and 'Hei tulkaa nopeesti' ('Hey come quickly'). She also asks several times if someone is already coming to help by saying, 'Onks joku tulossa jo' ('Is someone coming already'), 'Tuleeksielt kettää' ('Is anyone coming'), 'Onksielt tulos joku' ('Is someone coming from there'). In the beginning Auer is shouting but becomes calmer during the call. Auer was not at the victim's side because the phone was in the kitchen and the victim in the fireplace room being attacked by the killer. Auer, however, left the phone and attempted to go to the victim because she perhaps wanted to help him. When she returned to the phone, the first thing she said was, 'Mä yritän auttaa' ('I'm trying to help') followed by her question 'Onksielt tulos joku' ('Is someone coming from there'). The part 'Mä yritän auttaa' ('I'm trying to help') is based on my personal observation and also what Roosa Rentola related in her book '*Kielestä kiinni*' of having heard in the recording.

According to the study in the book '*Analyzing 911 Homicide Calls: Practical Aspects and Applications*', the following can be considered matters that indicate guilt of an emergency caller:

1) Defendant mentality. The caller denies that they are guilty of the act in any way.
2) Ingratiating remarks. This manifests as over-politeness, such as asking how the operator is doing or apologising during the call.
3) Insults or blames victim. This happens especially when it is related to unwillingness to help the victim.
4) Minimising. A guilty caller may openly minimise or diminish their own part in the situation, or the caller may attempt to create themselves an alibi by describing they have just arrived at the scene. This characteristic is particularly noteworthy if it appears in the beginning of the call.

5) Mental miscues. Freudian slips or non sequiturs may reveal matters that the caller did not want to tell. For example, the caller may accidentally tell something about the manner of death.

None of the above can be observed in Auer's speech in the recording. Rentola contemplated in her book that Auer's only politeness could be considered to be the goodbyes 'heihei' ('bye') she says at the end of the call. Santtila had thought about the same thing, in other words, if Auer was overly polite when using those words. However, according to the instructions of the evaluation form, it was unclear if also such expressions should be classified as politeness that were merely responses to the other person. Personally, I think 'heihei' ('bye') sounds like a common ending for a phone call, and I would not interpret it as being overly polite.

Even if many people have had the feeling from the emergency call that Auer is behaving in a somehow strange or unusual manner during the call and that it could be a sign of guilt, scientific research does not support this assumption. Instead, the result is quite the contrary, suggesting her innocence.

10. THE TRUTH ABOUT THE EMERGENCY CALL

Is everything a lie that is not true? In life, things are seldom black and white. A lot can remain between the truth and a lie. People can be honest but, in spite of that, what they say may not always be true because people forget and misremember, and can be ignorant. Facts may seem different from different points of view. People may exaggerate, diminish or otherwise distort things, which puts matters somewhere in the middle ground between the truth and the lie.

A lie is not always intentional, and people also make mistakes and errors. However, it is true that people, on occasion, lie entirely deliberately. People do not always consider lying as a bad thing: they may think their lying promotes a good objective, for example in capturing a criminal. I do not know about the motives of the police, but not all of the mistakes made in the Ulvila murder investigation can be considered unintentional, no matter how positively one would approach them. Part of them have been made entirely on purpose in order for the truth to appear in the way the police wanted it to appear.

Can even the expert statements be trusted? The sound analyst of the NBI Forensic Laboratory changed her perception of the contents of the emergency call recording several times or, should I say, always when necessary. At first, she heard all kinds of sounds of fighting and sounds made by an outside man in the background. When Auer was made a suspect, the sound analyst no longer heard any sounds at all that suggested an outside perpetrator. On the contrary, the analyst then stated that there could not possibly have been an outsider present on the basis of the recording. With the assistance of the police, she also found the two-syllable word '_(u)ole', which she had not heard before in the recording, uttered by Auer in a commanding tone.

When one of Auer's children reported almost five years after the murder that they had heard sounds of a cassette player and his father's cries as if they had started again exactly as they had first sounded at the beginning, the sound analyst stated it was possible that pre-recorded sounds had been played in the background of the emergency call. Nevertheless, the FBI did not find any signs of a premade recording present on the emergency call recording. When the conductor who had participated in the investigation told the sound analyst which part in the recording was proof of pre-recording, the sound analyst then agreed with the conductor, even though she had to change her previous perception of some of the sounds she had heard in the recording before.

The trustworthiness of expert statements cannot be evaluated merely on the basis that the expert is qualified to make a statement on a certain matter because of their position, education or experience. Experts are people and they may have the same weaknesses in relation to truth as anyone else. In addition to the qualifications of a person issuing a statement, attention should be paid to the reasoning of the conclusions when evaluating the trustworthiness of an expert statement.

Is the emergency call recording authentic? The emergency call no longer sounds as it sounded like on 1 December 2006 when Anneli Auer called the emergency response centre. The probative force of the emergency call recording is naturally poor if it no longer corresponds to the original. When doubts were raised as to the authenticity of the emergency call, the police claimed to have restored the original emergency call from the backup recording of the emergency response centre and found it was identical in its contents to the recording heard in the trials. Nevertheless, this could not be true. At that stage, restoring the emergency call from the emergency response centre was no longer even possible.

The change in the emergency call recording is small, only a few seconds in length, but it had a large impact. By using it, the police managed to get Auer to suspect her own recollection of the murder night and speculate a different course of events in the way desired by the police. The case was argued in every court instance and even if, according to the reasons for the judgments, Auer was never condemned specifically on the basis of the changed part of the emergency call recording, it has in part influenced the overall picture of the judges regarding the case. After all, judges are people like the rest of us.

APPENDICES

1. House plan by Matti Mäkinen, 11 December 2006.
2. Emergency call transcription by Tuija Niemi, 19 December 2006.
    -   This transcription corresponds to the transcription made by Niemi on 13 December 2006 with the exception of one correction. In the earlier version, one spoken line had been mistakenly attributed to the emergency response centre operator even though it had been spoken by Anneli Auer.
    -   This transcription was received by the defence in 2011 as part of the material of one of the further investigations, at the point when it was revealed that other transcriptions had been made in addition to the one presented by the police and prosecution. The date 04.04.11 (4 April 2011) refers to the date when the transcription was printed.
3. Emergency call transcription by Tuija Niemi, 28 August 2009.
    -   This transcription was made on 13 August 2009, and the different date supplied results from the fact that the transcription was delivered as an appendix to the statement given on 28 August 2009.
4. Emergency call transcription by Mika Sihvonen, 17 January 2008.

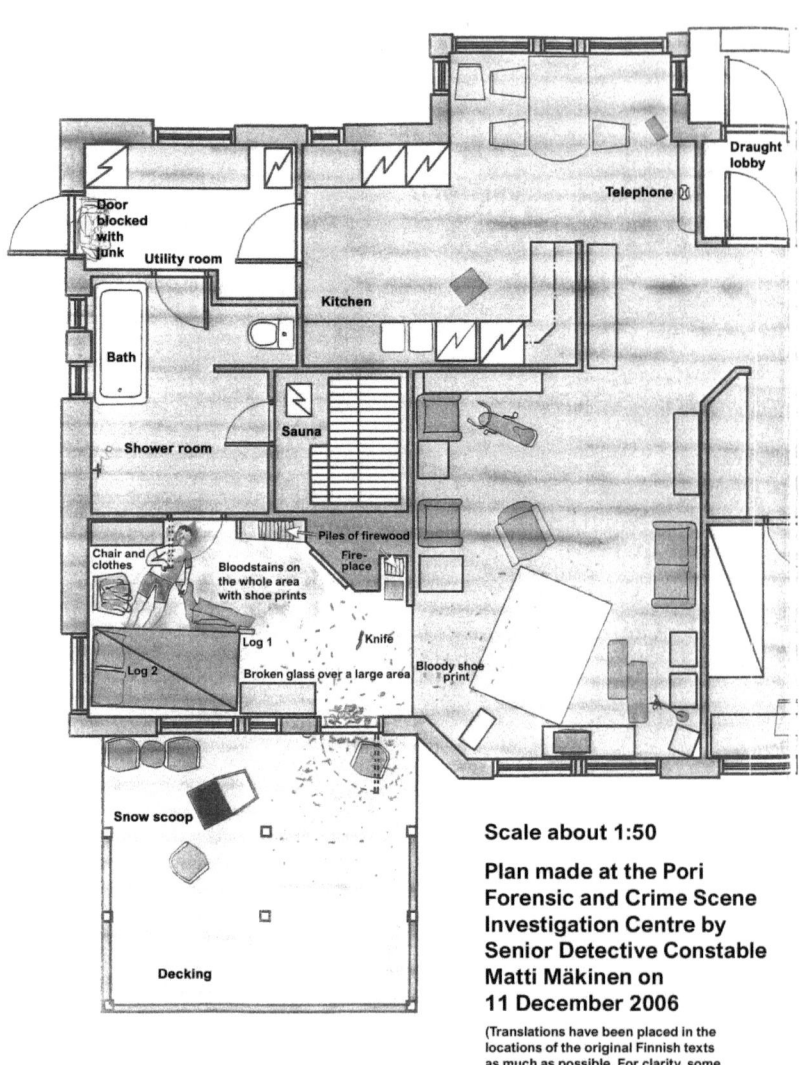

Draught lobby

Telephone

Door blocked with junk

Utility room

Kitchen

Bath

Sauna

Shower room

Piles of firewood

Chair and clothes

Fire-place

Bloodstains on the whole area with shoe prints

Log 1

Knife

Bloody shoe print

Log 2

Broken glass over a large area

Snow scoop

Decking

Scale about 1:50

Plan made at the Pori Forensic and Crime Scene Investigation Centre by Senior Detective Constable Matti Mäkinen on 11 December 2006

(Translations have been placed in the locations of the original Finnish texts as much as possible. For clarity, some texts have been placed fully on either the left or the right side of the plan.)

136

PLAN APPENDIX FOR INVESTIGATION REPORT 6580/R/16735/06

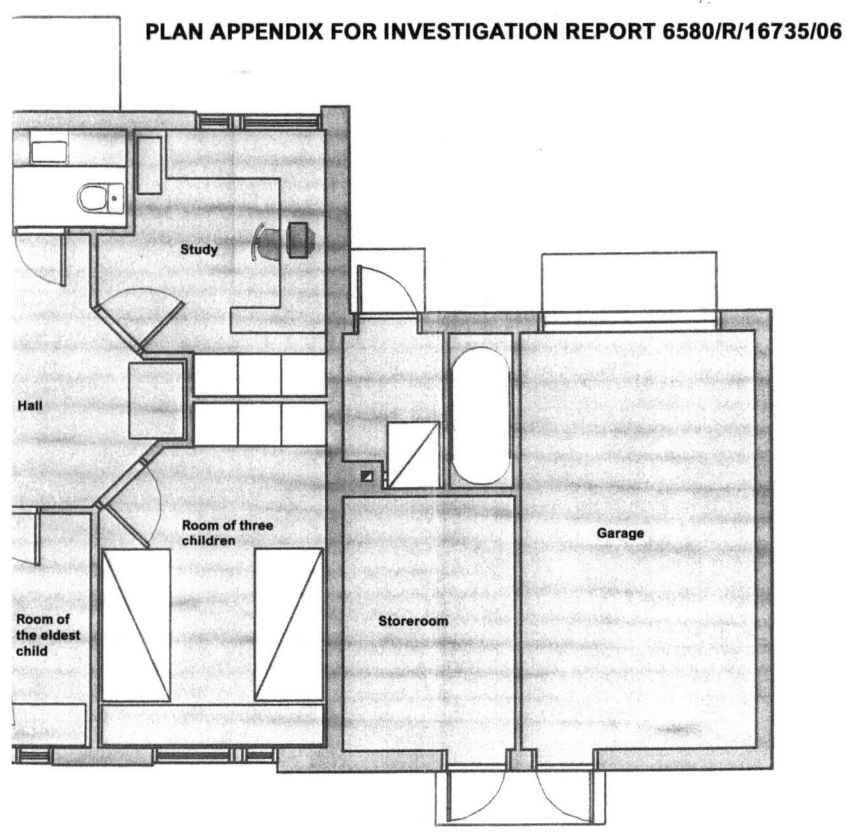

KRP	Näytteen sisältö kirjallisena	RTL 25661/4/06	LIITE
RTL	Näyte: 26 häken puhelu 1.12.2006	Sivu 1 (4)	
RLAB-ÄÄNI-2	6580/R/16735/06	04.04.11	

Korjattu versio 19.12.2006 kohta 1:41 repliikki/TNL

Puhujat

Häke
Nainen
Tyttö
Uhri
?Tekijä

Selvityksiä merkintöihin:

( )( )	epäselvät kohdat tai vaihtoehtoiset tulkinnat
...	kohdat joista ei saa selvää
Puhetta/	todettu repliikki (tauko seuraa)
/kommentti	kommentoidaan edellä olevaa puhetyyliä tms.
___	sanan sisällä oleva äänne, josta ei saa selvää
[ ]	muu kuin puheääni, esim. [kolahdus]

Äänitallenteen sisältö, näyte 26

Aika	Puhuja	Repliikki/kommentti
0:01	Häke	Hätäkeskus
0:02	Nainen	Tääl o joku tappaja/Tulkaa nopeesti/
0:04	Häke	Mi, mikä/
	Nainen	Joku tuli ikkunast sisää/
0:05	Häke	Rauhotu, mikä paikkakunta/
0:06	Nainen	Ulvila/
0:07	Häke	Ulvila, jooh/
0:10	Nainen	Tähtisentie viiskytneljä/
0:12	Häke	Anteeks mikä/
0:12	Nainen	Tähtisentie/
0:15	Häke	Joo-o/
0:15	Nainen	Viiskytneljä/
0:16	Häke	Onks tää omakotitalo/
0:17	Nainen	On/
0:17	Häke	Mitä siellä nyt tapahtuu/
0:19	Nainen	Joku tuli ikkunast sisää ja hakkaa puukol mun miestäni/Muaki on hakattu/
0:23	Häke	Joku hakkaa puukolla/
	Uhri	Auuu Aii
0:24	Nainen	Kyllä/
		Heti/
0:26	Häke	Kuka siel hakkaa puukolla, tunneksä sitä/
	Uhri	Auu/
0.:30	Nainen	Ei se o pimeetä/ Mä juoksi puhelimee ku mä pääsin/
		Löi muaki, tulee näköjää verta/

KESKUSRIKOSPOLIISI   Jokiniemenkuja 4   puh (09) 8388 661
RIKOSTEKNINEN LABORATORIO   01370 VANTAA   fax (09) 8388 6303

© Liitteen saa kopioida vain kokonaan.

54

KRP Näytteen sisältö kirjallisena RTL 25661/4/06 LIITE
RTL Näyte: 26 häken puhelu 1.12.2006 Sivu 2 (4)
RLAB-ÄÄNI-2 6580/R/16735/06 04.04.11

0:35	Häke	Joo/
	Nainen	Hei nopeesti/
0:37	Häke	Joo, laitan apua/ Onks teillä monta siellä/
0:39	Nainen	Meil o myös neljä lasta täällä/
0:41	Häke	Neljä lasta/
0:42	Nainen	Kyllä/*toteava, mutta ei huolestunut äänensävy*
0:43	Häke	Jaaha, odota hetki mä meen hetkeks pois linjalta/
		Älä sulje puhelinta, älä me pois/
	Uhri	Aihh/ *ininaä, valitusta*
0:47	Nainen	En/
0:50	Uhri	Aiii/
		[Laahaava ääni] *tuolin, sohvan tms. painavan esineen siirto, vai liikkuuko uhri?*
0:52	Nainen	Nopeesti/
0:53	Uhri	(Tuu jo)/
0:54	Nainen	Kuuleksä ku mun mieheni huutaa/
0:56	Uhri	[napsahdus] Öhh. [kolahdus] Ahh.
		lyödäänkö niin kovaa johonkin, että kuuluu kolahduksia, vai tuleeko äänet
		puhelinlinjasta vai liikkuuko uhri?
0:59	Nainen	Meni, lähtikse mies jo/ *kysyy ilmeisesti uhrilta, ei tytöltä*
1:01	Uhri	Aargh/ *erittäin voimakas karjaisu*
	Nainen	*hengittää raskaasti puhelimeen*
1:06	Uhri	(Äihh) (Häivy)/
		[Laahaava ääni] *tuolin, sohvan tms. painavan esineen siirto?*
		voi olla myös uhrin valitus-ääniä, ei saa selvää
1:06	Uhri	Äähh, Auuh/ *voimakkaita valitushuutoja*
1:12	Nainen	Onks joku tulossa jo/
1:15	Uhri	Öh/ ...auto/ Oh/ Eih/
1:25	Uhri	Hälytyys/
		(Juha)(kuka) tule(e) tänne apuun
1:34-	?	Tallennuksessa tyhjä kohta 2 sekunnin ajan
1:36		Mitä tapahtuu, koska järjestelmä reagoi kaikkeen ääneen, myös hengitykseen?
1:36	Nainen	Hei mun täytyy ny/ Amanda/
1:38	Tyttö	Niih/
1:39	Nainen	Tuuksä tänne puhelimee/
1:40	Uhri	Agh/
1:41	Nainen	Mä meen kattoo tonne/
1:42	Tyttö	Mitä mä sanon/
1:43	Nainen	Mä, mä soitan poliisil, siel pyydettii et/
1:46	Uhri	(pyyjääpää)/
1:46	Nainen	Mikä tota sen nimi o/ *sanoo kauempana puhelimesta, kysyykö uhrilta*
		mennessään lähemmäs?
1:48	Uhri	(No minä) ... autaa/
		(ännou)/ keskellä sanaa kuuluu [napsahdus]
1:51	Nainen	Lähtikse jo/ *kuuluu hiljempana kuin uhrin ääni*
1:52	Uhri	Tu(l)e auttaa/
1:54	Nainen	Mitäkö/ *huutaa raivokkaasti*

55

KRP   Näytteen sisältö kirjallisena   RTL 25661/4/06   LIITE
RTL   Näyte: 26 häken puhelu 1.12.2006   Sivu 3 (4)
RLAB-ÄÄNI-2   6580/R/16735/06   04.04.11

1:55	Uhri	Yöh/ *yokkailee*
	TAI	
	?Tekijä	Lyöh/
1:55	Nainen	Vittikö/
		[rapinaa, juoksuaskelia] *juoksevatko tekijä ja nainen?*
2:00	Uhri	Aagh/ *valittaa*
2:02	Uhri	A-laalalala/ lala *ei pysty enää puhumaan selvästi*
	Nainen	.../2-tavuinen sana, ei saa selvää, päällekkäin miehen valituksen kanssa
	Nainen	Öh/ *voimakkaan ponnistuksen aiheuttama äännähdys, siirtääkö uhria?*
2:08	Nainen	Tuleeksielt kettää/ *tulee puhumaan puhelimen lähelle*
2:10	Tyttö	Hei, onksiel joku, tulkaa äkkii, mun iskä voi huonosti/
		Tulkaa äkkii/ *taustalla uhrin valitusta*
2:17	?Uhri	...(n)ui *vaa/erittäin vaimea ääni*
	?Tekijä	
2:19	Tyttö	Iskä, älä kuole/
2:22	Uhri	Aiih/
	Nainen	Hei, lopeta/ *huutaa tekijälle*
2:25		[rapinaa, mahdollisesti askelien ääniä] tms.
	?Uhri	(Aja)/
2:26	Häke	Joo haloo/
2:27	Uhri?	(se jäi)/
	Tyttö	Nii tulkaa äkkii, mun iskä voi huonosti, jooko/
		taustalla kamppailun ääniä, uhrin valituksia
2:31	Häke	Joo, sinne on apu jo tulossa/ Osaakko sä, onks siel joku aikuinen paikalla nytte/
2:35	Tyttö	Äiti/
2:36	Häke	Voisko äiti puhuu/
2:38	Tyttö	Äiti, tuu/
2:39		[voimakas kolahdus] *oveen tai lattiaan hakkaaminen, vai hakataanko uhria?*
2:39	Tyttö	Nyt siel puhutaa taas/
2:41		[metallinen ääni + vaimea kolahdus] *omituinen ääni kauempana taustalla?*
2:42	Nainen	..Onksielt tulos joku/ *puhelimessa*
2:44	Häke	Joo, mä oon apuu hälyttäny/Mä voidaan nyt, mä vähän kyselen lisätietoja/
		[metallinen ääni] *omituinen ääni kauempana taustalla, samankalt. kuin 2:41?*
		Mikä on tilanne nyt, apu on on koko ajan tulossa/
2:50	Nainen	Joo/ Mä en tiedä mikä tyyppi se o, se/
	?Tekijä	.../ *kuulostaa miehen ääneltä. uhri?, häken taustalta?, jää naisen repliikin alle*
2:52	Nainen	Hajotti meiän ton, se taka-ovi, sil o mustat vaatteet/
2:56	Häke	Jo, onks hän siel paikal viel/
2:58	Nainen	Mä olen tääl, mä juoksin äske ulos, et mä meen sinne, se lähtee juoksee mun
		perää/
		Se meni takas ja se aikoo tappaa mun mieheni, se oli äske viel hengis/
3:06	Häke	Joo, missä se sun mies, mimmoses tilas se sun mies siel nyt on/
3:10	Nainen	Makaa siel lattial ja huus äske apua, nyt hiljeni/
3:14	Häke	Sun mies hiljeni vai/
3:14	Tyttö	itkun alkua + voimakas rääkäisy
3:17	Häke	Haloo/

56

KRP	Näytteen sisältö kirjallisena	RTL 25661/4/06	LIITE
RTL	Näyte: 26 häken puhelu 1.12.2006	Sivu 4 (4)	
RLAB-ÄÄNI-2	6580/R/16735/06	04.04.11	

3:18	Nainen	Älä itke Amanda hei, siel/
3:21	Häke	Joo, sinne on apu koko ajan tulossa, onks sun mies nyt iha tiedottomana makaa vai/ *tyttö itkee taustalla*
3:25	Nainen	Emmä tiedä, mä en oo, keittiös, mä en/ Meneks mä kattomaa/
3:30	Häke	Joo, mut missäs se tekijä nyt on, missä se tekijä täl hetkel on/
3:33	nainen	No todennäkösest siel ellei lähteny ulos jo, mei makuuhuoneessa siis/
3:36	Häke	Lähti ulos jo vai/
3:37	Nainen	En tiedä, siel hiljeni/
3:39	Häke	Jaaha/
	Nainen	Amanda oliks se viel siel/
3:41	Tyttö	Joo, se lähti/
3:42	Nainen	Se lähti jo vai/
3:43	Häke	Sano vähä tuntomerkkejä, mä voin sanoo poliisille, mustat vaatteet ja mitä muuta/
3:47	Nainen	Mustat vaatteet, siin oli joku, sanotaa et vähintää 180 senttii pitkä, vähä, aika tukeva/
3:53	Häke	Joo/
3:54	Nainen	Semmoset niiku mustat vaatteet, semmoset, ettei naamaa kokonaa näkyny/ Iha vieraan näköne mulle/
3:58	Häke	Iha vieras/
3:59	Nainen	Jooh/ *taustalta kuuluu tytön itkua* Hei tulkaa nopeesti/
4:02	Häke	Joo, poliisi soittaa sul, me voidaan lopettaa sitte/
4:05	Nainen	Onks tänne joku ambulanssi tulossa kans/
4:07	Häke	On ambulanssi on kans tulossa ja poliisi, mut me voidaan lopettaa ni poliisi soittaa/
4:11	Nainen	Joo/
4:12	Häke	Täst tavottaa täst sun numerosta, mistä sä soitat nyt/ *tyttö itkee taustalla* Me voidaan lopettaa, poliisi soittaa/
4:16	Nainen	Joo/ Selvä/
4:17	Häke	Joo, hei/
4:18	Nainen	Heihei/
		Tallennus päättyy.

5 7

KRP   Näytteen sisältö kirjallisena   RTL 25651/35/05   LIITE
RTL   Näyte: 26 häken puhelu 1.12.2006   Sivu 1 (5)
RLAB-ÄÄNI-2 6580/R/16735/06   28.08.09

Puhujat   Häke   Hätäkeskus
                     Anneli   Soittaja
                     Amanda Tyttö
                     Jukka   Uhri taustalla

Selvityksiä merkintöihin:

         ( )( )   epäselvät kohdat tai vaihtoehtoiset tulkinnat
         ...   kohdat joista ei saa selvää
         Puhetta/   todettu repliikki (tauko seuraa)
         /kommentti   kommentoidaan edellä olevaa puhetyyliä tms.
                        sanan sisällä oleva äänne, josta ei saa selvää
         [ ]   muu kuin puheääni, esim. [kolahdus]

Äänitallenteen sisältö, näyte 26, puhelu alkaa klo 02:43:21

rivi	Aika	Todaika	Puhuja	Repliikki/kommentti
1	0:01	02:43:22	Häke	Hätäkeskus
2	0:02	02:43:23	Anneli	Tääl o joku tappaja/ Tulkaa nopeesti/
3	0:04	02:43:25	Häke	Mi, mikä/
			Anneli	Joku tuli ikkunast sisää/
4	0:05		Häke	Rauhotu, mikä paikkakunta/
5	0:06		Anneli	Ulvila/
6	0:07		Häke	Ulvila, jooh/
7	0:10		Anneli	Tähtisentie viiskytneljä/
8	0:12		Häke	Anteeks mikä/
9	0:12		Anneli	Tähtisentie/
10	0:15		Häke	Joo-o/
11	0:15		Anneli	Viiskytneljä/
12	0:16		Häke	Onks tää omakotitalo/
13	0:17		Anneli	On/
14	0:17		Häke	Mitä siellä nyt tapahtuu/
15	0:19	02:43:40	Anneli	Joku tuli ikkunast sisää ja hakkaa puukol mun miestäni/ Muaki on hakattu/
16	0:23		Häke	Joku hakkaa puukolla/
			Jukka	Auuu/
17	0:24		Anneli	Kyllä/ Heti/
18			Jukka	Annuu/
19	0:26		Häke	Kuka siel hakkaa puukolla, tunneksä sitä/
			Jukka	Auu/
20	0:30	02:43:51	Anneli	Ei se o pimeetä/ Mä juoksi puhelimee ku mä pääsin/ Löi muaki, tulee näköjää verta/

KESKUSRIKOSPOLIISI   Jokiniemenkuja 4   puh. (09) 8388 661
RIKOSTEKNINEN LABORATORIO   01370 VANTAA   fax (09) 8388 6303

KRP   Näytteen sisältö kirjallisena   RTL 25661/35/06   LIITE
RTL   Näyte: 26 häken puhelu 1.12.2006   Sivu 2 (5)
RLAB-ÄÄNI-2   6580/R/16735/06   28.08.09

21	0:35		Häke	Joo/
			Anneli	Hei nopeesti/
22	0:37		Häke	Joo, laitan apua/ Onks teillä monta siellä/
23	0:39		Anneli	Meil o myös neljä lasta täällä/
24	0:41		Häke	Neljä lasta/
25	0:42		Anneli	Kyllä/
26	0:43	02:44:04	Häke	Jaaha, odota hetki mä meen hetkeks pois linjalta/
				Älä sulje puhelinta, älä me pois/
			Jukka	Aihh/*yninää, valitusta*
27	0:47		Anneli	En/
28	0:50	02:44:11	Jukka	Aiii/
				[Laahaava ääni]
29	0:52	02:44:13	Anneli	Nopeesti/
30	0:53		Jukka	(Tuu jo)(huijaa)/
31	0:54	02:44:15	Anneli	Kuuleksä ku mun mieheni huutaa/
32	0:56		Jukka	[napsahdus] Öhh/
				[kolahdus] Ähh/
33	0:59	02:44:20	Anneli	Meni, lähtikse mies jo/
34	1:01		Jukka	Aargh/
				erittäin voimakas karjaisu
35			Anneli	*hengittää raskaasti puhelimeen*
36	1:06	02:44:27		(Äihh) (Häivy)/ käheä rääkäisy
			Jukka	[Laahaava ääni]
				Äähh, Auuh/
				voimakkaita valitushuutoja
37	1:12	02:44:33	Anneli	Onks joku tulossa jo/
38	1:15		Jukka	Öh/
39			Jukka	...auto/
40			Jukka	Oh/ Eih/
41	1:25		Jukka	Hälytyys/
				... tule(e) tänne apuun/
42	1:34-1:36			Tallennuksessa tyhjä kohta 2 sekunnin ajan
				Mitä tapahtuu, koska järjestelmä reagoi kaikkeen ääneen,
				myös hengitykseen?
43	1:36	02:44:57	Anneli	Hei mun täytyy ny/ Amanda/
44	1:38		Amanda	Niih/
45	1:39	02:45:00	Anneli	Tuuksä tänne puhelimee/
46	1:40		Jukka	Agh/ *valittaa*
47	1:41		Anneli	Mä meen kattoo tonne/
48	1:42		Amanda	Mitä mä sanon/
49	1:43	02:45:04	Anneli	Mä, mä soitan poliisil, siel pyydettii et/
50	1:46		Jukka	(pyyjääpää)/
51	1:46	02:45:07	?	(Mite mä pääse linjoi)/
				Tämä repliikki ei kuulosta naisen eikä tytön sanomalta,
				kuuluuko HÄKESTÄ?
52	1:48		Jukka	(No vähä voit auttaakii)/

KRP   Näytteen sisältö kirjailisena   RTL 25661/35/06   LIITE
RTL   Näyte: 26 häken puhelu 1.12.2006   Sivu 3 (5)
RLAB-ÄÄNI-2   6580/R/16735/06   28.08.09

				(Kylhän nous)/ *keskellä sanaa kuuluu [napsahdus]*
53	1:51	02:45:12	Anneli	Lähtikse jo/ *kuuluu hiljempana kuin Jukan ääni*
54	1:52		Jukka	Tu(l)e auttaa/
55	1:54	02:45:15	Anneli	(Mitäkö)(pitääkö)/ *huutaa raivokkaasti*
56	1:55		Jukka	Yöh/ *yökkäilee* *ähkäisy*
57	1:55	02:45:16	Anneli	Vittikö/ [juoksuaskelia] [oven aukaisu]
58	2:00		Jukka	Aagh/ *valittaa*
59	2:02	02:45:23	Jukka	A-laalalala/ *ei pysty enää puhumaan selvästi* [kopsahdus] *keskellä*
60	2:03- 2:04	02:45:24	Anneli	(_uole)/*2-tavuinen sana, päällekkäin miehen valituksen kanssa*
61	2:05	02:45:26	Jukka Anneli	[vaimea kopsahdus] Lala/ Öh/ *voimakkaan ponnistuksen aiheuttama äännähdys*
62	2:07		Anneli	.../
63	2:08	02:45:29	Anneli	[vaimeita askeleita] Tuleeksielt kettää/
64	2:10		Amanda	Hei, onksiel joku, tulkaa äkkii, mun iskä voi huonosti/ Tulkaa äkkii/ *taustalla Jukan valitusta*
65	2:17		?	...(n)ui vaa/*erittäin vaimea ääni*
66	2:19		Amanda	Iskä, älä kuole/
67	2:22	02:45:43	Jukka	Aiih/
68	2:23	02:45:44	Anneli	Hei, lopeta/ *huutaa todella raivokkaasti*
69	2:25		?	[askelien ääniä] (Aja).../
70	2:26	02:45:47	Häke	Joo haloo/
71	2:27	02:45:48	Jukka Amanda	(se jäi)/ Nii tulkaa äkkii, mun iskä voi huonosti, jooko/ *Jukan valituksia*
72	2:31	02:45:52	Häke	Joo, sinne on apu jo tulossa/ Osaakko sä, onks siel joku aikuinen paikalla nytte/
73	2:32	02:45:53		*Jukan puheääntä ei enää kuulu*
74	2:35		Amanda	Äiti/
75	2:36	02:45:57	Häke	Voisko äiti puhuu/
76	2:38		Amanda	Äiti, tuu/
77	2:39	02:46:00		[kolahdus]
78	2:39		Amanda	Nyt siel puhutaa taas/
79	2:41	02:46:02		[metallinen ääni + vaimeampi kolahdus]
80	2:42	02:46:03	Anneli	Onksielt tulos joku/
81	2:44		Häke	Joo, mä oon apuu hälyttäny/ Mä voidaan nyt, mä vähän kyselen lisätietoja/ Mikä on tilanne nyt, apu on on koko ajan tulossa/
82	2:50	02:46:11	Anneli	Joo/ Mä en tiedä mikä tyyppi se o, se/
83	2:52		Anneli	Hajotti meiän ton, se taka-ovi, sil o mustat vaatteet/

KRP
RTL
RLAB-ÄÄNI-2

Näytteen sisältö kirjallisena
Näyte: 26 häken puhelu 1.12.2006
6580/R/16735/06

RTL 25661/35/06
Sivu 4 (5)
28.08.09

LIITE

84	2:56		Häke	Jo, onks hän siel paikal viel/
85	2:58		Anneli	Mä olen tääl, mä juoksin äske ulos, et mä meen sinne, se lähtee juoksee mun perää/ Se meni takas ja se aikoo tappaa mun mieheni, se oli äske viel hengis/
86	3:06		Häke	Joo, missä se sun mies, mimmoses tilas se sun mies siel nyt on/
87	3:10	02:46:31	Anneli	Makaa siel lattial ja huus äske apua, nyt hiljeni/
88	3:14		Häke	Sun mies hiljeni vai/
89	3:14	02:46:35	Amanda	itkun alkua + voimakas rääkäisy [lyhyt napsahdus]
90	3:17		Häke	Haloo/
91	3:18		Anneli	Älä itke Amanda hei, siel/
92	3:21		Häke	Joo, sinne on apu koko ajan tulossa, onks sun mies nyt iha tiedottomana makaa vai/ Amanda itkee taustalla
93	3:25		Anneli	Emmä tiedä, mä en oo, keittiös, mä en/ Meneks mä kattomaa/
94	3:30		Häke	Joo, mut missäs se tekijä nyt on, missä se tekijä täl hetkel on/
95	3:33		Anneli	No todennäkösest siel ellei lähteny ulos jo, mei makuuhuoneessa siis/
96	3:36		Häke	Lähti ulos jo vai/
97	3:37		Anneli	En tiedä, siel hiljeni/
98	3:39	02:47:00	Häke Anneli	Jaaha/ Amanda oliks se viel siel/
99	3:41		Amanda	Joo, se lähti/
100	3:42		Anneli	Se lähti jo vai/
101	3:43		Häke	Sano vähä tuntomerkkejä, mä voin sanoo poliisille, mustat vaatteet ja mitä muuta/
102	3:47		Anneli	Mustat vaatteet, siin oli joku, sanotaa et vähintää 180 senttii pitkä, vähä, aika tukeva/
103	3:53		Häke	Joo/
104	3:54	02:47:15	Anneli	Semmoset niiku mustat vaatteet, semmoset, ettei naamaa kokonaa näkyny/Iha vieraan näköne mulle/
105	3:58		Häke	Iha vieras/
106	3:59		Anneli	Jooh/ taustalta kuuluu Amandan itkua Hei tulkaa nopeesti/
107	4:02		Häke	Joo, poliisi soittaa sul, me voidaan lopettaa sitte/
108	4:05	02:47:26	Anneli	Onks tänne joku ambulanssi tulossa kans/
109	4:07		Häke	On ambulanssi on kans tulossa ja poliisi, mut me voidaan lopettaa ni poliisi soittaa/
110	4:11		Anneli	Joo/
111	4:12		Häke	Täst tavottaa täst sun numerosta, mistä sä soitat nyt/ Amanda itkee taustalla Me voidaan lopettaa, poliisi soittaa/
112	4:16		Anneli	Joo/ Selvä/
113	4:17		Häke	Joo, hei/

KRP   Näytteen sisältö kirjallisena   RTL 25561/35/06   LIITE
RTL   Näyte: 26 häken puhelu 1.12.2006   Sivu 5 (5)
RLAB-ÄÄNI-2 6580/R/16735/06   28.08.09

114	4:18		Anneli	Heihei/
				Tallennus päättyy.

34

Nauhoitteen analysointiraportti

Hätäkeskuksen 1.12.2006 tallentamaa nauhoitetta analysointiin Tampereen yliopiston hypermedialaboratorion studiotilassa 11., 15. ja 17. tammikuuta 2008. Analysointiin käytettiin äänenkäsittelyohjelmistoja Sound Forge 9.0 sekä Audacity. Kuuntelulaitteistona käytössä oli lisäksi Genelec-kaiuttimet ja AKG-kuulokkeet.

USB-muistiin on tallennettu muutamia tehostettuja versioita alkuperäisestä ÄÄNI.WAV - tiedosta. Analysointi ja litterointi tehtiin pitkälti sound_dynamic_27db.wav -version avulla, jossa äänen dynamiikkaa on tehostettu siten, että taustan hiljaisemmat äänet voimistuvat huomattavasti suhteessa voimakkaampiin ääniin, kuten varsinaiseen puhelinkeskusteluun. Samoin yksittäiset kolahdukset ja mahdolliset tekijän äänet on voimistettu samalla tavoin, lisäksi USB-muistilla on versioita, jossa ääntä on hidastettu time strech -työkalun avulla siten, että äänen korkeus ja sävy pysyy alkuperäisen kaltaisena. Lisäksi muokatut äänet on prosessoitu taajuuskorjaimen avulla, jolloin äänestä saadaan muun muassa häivytettyä häiritseviä ääniä.

Kaikki edellä mainitut toimenpiteet saattavat kuitenkin oleellisesti muuttaa alkuperäisen äänen luonnetta siten, että esimerkiksi puhujan puheääni muuttuu huomattavasti. Tällöin tarkoituksen onkin ollut lähinnä keskittyä esimerkiksi äännähdyksen mahdolliseen verbaaliseen sisältöön, eikä niinkään auditiiviseen kokonaisasuun. Tämä on esimerkiksi kyseessä äänitiedostossa tekija_0107 slow.wav.

Tampereella 17.11.2008

Yliassistentti, FL
Mika Sihvonen
Hypermedialaboratorio
Tampereen yliopisto

58

147

TALLENNE 1.12.2006

N=Nainen, U=uhri, Hk=hätäkeskus

aika:	puhelinkeskustelu + keittiön äänet	makuuhuone + etäisempi häly	muuta:
00:00	- N: Ähhh! - Hk: Hätäkeskus - N: Tääl on joku tappaja, tulkaa nopeesti! - Hk: Mikä paik.. - N: Joku tuli ikkunast sisään...! - Hk: Rauhotu, mikä paikkakunta? - N: Ulvila! - Hk: Ulvila, joo? - N: Tähtisentie viiskytneljä! - Hk: Anteeks, mikä - N: Tähtisentie.	- [Uhri: Äääh] - [Uhri: An-aa]	[Hk: näppäimistön ääntä]
00:15	- Hk: Joo. - N: 54. - Hk: Onks tää omakotitalo? - N: On. - Hk: Joo, mitä siellä nyt tapahtuu? - N: Joku tuli ikkunast sisään ja hakkaa puukolla mun miestäni, muakin on hakattu. - Hk: Joku hakkaa puukolla... - N: Kyllä - Hk: (Kuka) siellä hakkaa puukolla? - N: Heti - Hk: Kuka siellä hakkaa puukolla?	- [Uhri: An-aa] - [Uhri: Ei-Auuu!] - [Uhri: Ann!] - [Uhri: Älä-Auuu!]	

59

00:30	- Hk: Tunneksä sitä?		
	- N: E, Ei, siel on pimeetä mä juoksin		'
	puhelimeen, ku mä pääsin... ...mullei,		
	mullakin tulee näköjään verta...		
	- Hk: Joo, joo.		00:40
	- N: Hei nopeesti!		[mahd.
	- Hk: Laitetaan apua, onks teitä monta	- [mahd.tekijän ääni: Uh]	makuuhuone]
	siellä?		Kolahdus/askel
	- N: Meil on myös neljä lasta täällä.		+uhrin ääni +
	- Hk: Neljä lasta?	- [Uhri: Nnuu!]	puuriman lyöntiä
	- N: Kyllä.		muistuttava ääni
	- Hk: Jaaha.		
00:45	- Hk: Odota hetki, mä meen hetkeks pois		[Hk: näppäimistön
	linjoilta, älä sulje puhelinta. Älä mee pois.		ääntä]
	- N: En.		[väh. 4
			juoksuaskelta]
		- [Uhri: Aiiii!]	[Huonekalun
	- N: Nopeesti!		raahausäänen
		- [Uhri: Tuu-joo!]	tyyppinen]
	- N: Ku-kuulek sä, kun mun mieheni	- [Uhri: Aah!]	
	huutaa!?	- [Uhri: Äh!]	
01:00	- N: Menik... lähtik se mies jo?	- [mahd. tekijän ääni:	
		Räh,]	
		- [Uhri: AA-AAAA!]	
		- [mahd. tekijän ääni:	[nopea sarja, mahd
		Rreeeihhh...]	askeleita]
		(ajassa 01:07)	
		- [Uhri: ee-oo!]	[huonekalun siirto
			ensimmäisen uhrin
			huudon jälkeen]
			[kovempi kolahdus
		- [Uhri: Ja-aaaa!]	ennen viimeistä
			huutoa ja mahd.
	- O-onks joku tulossa jo?		askeleita]
		- [Uhri: JA-AAAA!]	
		- [mahd.tekijän ääni:	
		TU!] (ajassa 01:15)	

60

01:15		- [Uhri: Äh!] - [Uhri: Auto/aalto] - [Uhri: Oh! Äh!] - [Uhri: AN-Nuuyyy!]	[kaksi: naksausta] [raahaus/ hankausäänen tyyppinen voimakkaampi ääni]
01:30	- N: Hei mun täytyy n... Amanda! - tytär: Ni! - N: Tuuk sä tänne puhelimeen, mä meen kattoo tonne. - tytär: Mitä mä sanon... - N: Mä, mä soitan poliisil, siel pyydettiin et...	- [Uhri: TULEE, TULE TÄNNE ANNUU!] - [Uhri: Uuh!] - [Uhri: Uu- uh!]	[Nauhoituksessa tauko 1.34 - 1.36]
01:45	- N: Miten mä pääsen linjoo? - [N: Lähtiks se jo?] - N: MITÄ SÄ!!? - N: Vittikö!!!	- [Uhri: TUU JO; TÄÄ!] - [Uhri: (No lähe) auttaan, Annuu!] - [Uhri: Tule auttaan!] [Tekijän ääni, "Ähkäisy" 01.56]	[mahdollinen sarja askeleita] [8 askelta]

- 61

02:00	- N: [Nyykäisy puhelimeen]	- [Uhri: O-Aauu!] - [Uhri: Aauuaa-aaa!]	- [Tytär: ketä siellä on?]
		- [Uhri: Aa!] - [Uhri: Aa!]	[voimakas kopsahdus, jonka jälkeen uhrin huudot]
	- N. Tuleek siält kettään?	- [Uhri: Aa!]	
	- Tytär: Hei onks siäl joku, tulkaa äkkii mun iskä voi huonosti!	- [Uhri: Ah!] - [Uhri: Aaaah!]	[4 napsausta, mahdollisesti hätäkeskuksen ääniä]
02:15	- Tytär: Tulkaa äkkii!!	- [Uhri: Aa!] - [Uhri: Kylmää]	[2 napsausta, mahdollisesti
	- Tytär: Iiii!		hätäkeskuksen ääniä]
	- Tytär: Eii!, Iskä älä kuole!	- [Uhri: Ni]	
	- N: HEI LOPETA!!!		[pieni kolahdus,
		- [a-jaa] (kuuluu askelsarjan aikana, joko	(mahd. esineen putoaminen) 02.24]
	- Hk: Joo haloo?	uhrin tai tekijän ääni)	[Nopeita askelia 8 kpl, 02.25]
	- Tytär: Ni, tulkaa äkkii mun iskä voi huonosti, jooko!	- [Uhri: A-jaa!] (uhrin viimeinen selkeästi tunnistettava ääni 02.28)	[5. askeleen kohdalla voimakkaampi kolahdus] [Voimakas kolahdus, 02.29, jonka jälkeen uhrin ääntä ei kuulu nauhalla.] (mahdollisesti lyönnin ubtaudacca

62

02:30	- Hk: Joo, tää... sinne on apu jo tulossa osaatko sä... onks siel jo aikuinen paikalla nytte...		
	- Tytär: Äiti.	- [mahd.tekijän ääni: hä]	
	- Hk: Voisko äiti puhuu?	(02.38)	[Voimakas kolahdus, 02.39]
	- Tytär: Äiti tuu.		[Toinen hiljaisempi
	- Tytär: Nyt siel puhutaan taas		kolahdus, jossa metallinen jälkikaiku,
	- N: Ei saa... aut.. onks sielt tulos joku!?		02.42]
02:45	- Hk: Joo mä oon apua hälyyttäny, mä... voidaan nyt... mä vähän kyselen lisätietoja.		(02:44 alkaen todennäköisesti hätäkeskuksen radioliikennettä tms. taustaääntä, hyvin etäistä keskustelua)
	- N: Joo.		[Yleisen hätämerkin tyyppinen korkea
	- Hk: Mikä siel on tilanne? Apu on kokoajan tulossa.		ääni taustalla] [02:46 mahdollisesti kevyt kolahdus
	- N: Mä en tiedä mikä tyyppi se on se... Hajotti meidän ton...		makuuhuoneesta]
	- Hk: Ni		[02:50 hätäkeskuksen taustalla: A-tah]
	- N: Se, takaovi... sill on mustat, mustat vaatteet...		
	- Hk: Joo, onks hän siel paikalla viel?		
	- N: Mä olen tääl, mä juoksin äsken...		

63

03:00	- Hk: Joo		[Näppäimistön ääntä hätäkeskuksesta]
	- N: ...Ulos, jos mä meen sinne se lähtee juokseen mun perään, se meni takasin, se aikoo tappaa mun mieheni, se oli äsken viäl hengis.		
	- Hk: Joo, misä se sun mies, mimmosessa tilassa se sun mies siel nyt on?		
	- N: Makaa siel lattialla ja huus äsken apu ... Nyt hiljeni!		
	- Hk: Sun mies hiljeni vai?		
03:15	- Hk: Haloo?	[Tytär kirkuu ja luultavasi lämäyttää käsillään, 03.16]	[keskustelun ääntä mahd. hätäkeskuksesta]
	- N: Älä itke Amanda, siel... (Nyyhkäisy)		
	- Hk: Joo, sinne on apua kokoajan tulossa, eli onks sun mies siellä nyt ihan tiedottomana makaa vai?		
	- N: Mä en tiä, mä en oo keittiös, mä e... meneks mä kattomaan?		
03:30	- Hk: Joo, mut misäs se tekijä nyt on, misäs se tekijä täl hetkel on?		
	- N: No todennäköisesti siel, ellei lähteny ulos jo. Meidän makuuhuoneessa siis.		
	- Hk: Lähti ulos jo vai?		
	- N: En tiedä, siel hiljeni, Amanda oliks se viel siäl?		

64

153

- Tytär: Ei, se lähti. - N: Se lähti jo vai. - Hk: Joo, mut sano vähän tuntomerkkejä mä voin sanoo poliisille,		[radioliikennettä tms. keskustelua 03:44]
03:45 - Hk: Mustat vaatteet ja mitä muuta... - N: Mustat vaatteet, semmonen joku... Emmä täält, vähintään satakahdeksankymment senttii pitkä, vähä, aika tukeva. - Hk: Joo. - N: Ja semmoset, niiku mustat vaatteet, semmot ettei naamaa ihan kokonaan näkyny, ihan vieraan näkönen mulle. - Hk: Ihan vieras... - N: Joo.		[radioliikennettä taustalla tms.]
4:00 -Hk: Joo. - N: Tulkaa nopeesti! - Hk: Joo. Poliisi soittaa sulle, me voidaan lopettaa sitte. - N: Onks teil joku ambulanssi tulossa kans? - Hk: On, ambulanssi on tulossa kans ja poliisi, mut me voidaan lopettaa ni poliisi soittaa.	[tytär nyyhkyttää taustalla]	

65